This book is part of the Victor FAMILY CONCERN SERIES, a multivolume library dealing with the major questions confronting Christian families today. Each book is accompanied by a Leader's Guide for group study and a Personal Involvement Workbook for individual enrichment. All are written in a readable practical style by qualified, practicing professionals. Authors of the series are:

Anthony Florio, Ph.D., premarriage, marriage, and family counselor, *Two to Get Ready* (premarital preparation);

Rex Johnson, assistant professor of Christian education, Talbot Seminary, active in pastoral counseling, *At Home with Sex* (sex education and marriage preparation in the family);

Harold Myra, publisher of *Christianity Today, Love Notes to Jeanette* (sexuality and fulfillment in marriage);

J. Allan Petersen, speaker at Family Affair Seminars, *Conquering Family Stress* (facing family crises);

Nancy Potts, marriage and family counselor, *Loneliness: Living Between the Times* (dealing with personal loneliness);

Wayne Rickerson, family pastor, Beaverton Christian Church, Beaverton, Oregon and director of Creative Home Teaching Seminars, *Family Fun and Togetherness* (family togetherness activities);

Barbara Sroka, served on research and writing committees with Chicago's Circle Church and is active with their single adults, *One Is a Whole Number* (singles and the church);

James Thomason, assistant pastor at Calvary Baptist Church, Detroit, *Common Sense about Your Family Dollars* (family finances);

Ted Ward, Ph.D., professor and director of Values Development Education program at Michigan State University, *Values Begin at Home* (value development in the family);

H. Norman Wright, assistant professor of psychology at Biola College and marriage, family, and child counselor, *The Family that Listens* (parent-child communication).

Consulting editor for the series is **J. Allan Petersen,** president of Family Concern Inc.

CONQUERING FAMILY STRESS

J. Allan Petersen

While this book is designed for the reader's personal enjoyment and profit, it is also intended for group study. A Leader's Guide with Victor Multiuse Transparency Masters and a Personal Involvement Workbook are available from your local Christian bookstore or from the publisher.

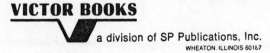

VICTOR BOOKS
a division of SP Publications, Inc.
WHEATON. ILLINOIS 60187

Offices also in Fullerton, California • Whitby, Ontario, Canada • Amersham-on-the-Hill, Bucks, England

Fourth printing, 1981

All Scripture quotations are taken from the King James Version.

Dewey Decimal Classification: 261.83427
        Subject headings: FAMILY; FAMILY RELATIONS; HOME LIFE

Library of Congress Catalog Card Number: 78-056625
ISBN: 0-88207-632-9

VICTOR BOOKS
A division of SP Publications, Inc.
P. O. Box 1825 ● Wheaton, Illinois 60187

Contents

Foreword

J. Allan Petersen is founder and president of Family Concern, Incorporated. He travels widely conducting marriage and family seminars. Among his books are The Marriage Affair, For Men Only, For Women Only, *and* For Families Only.

This book is a significant part of Victor Books' Family Concern Series. In a time of great family consciousness and opportunity, many congregations are devoting increasing energies to family ministries. They have requested reliable and practical resources that speak to the needs of contemporary families. Victor Books and Family Concern have shared this vision and have cooperatively developed this comprehensive family ministry resource for churches.

The church relates to people throughout their lives, and so can help them whatever their point of need. It can teach people skills and concepts for healthy marriage and family relationships with greater depth than any other institution. The church can offer assistance and support at times of crisis, and has built-in structures for education, enrichment, and problem-solving.

This Family Concern Series has been carefully planned to capitalize on the unique abilities and opportunities churches have to minister to families. These 12 books are an encyclopedia of practical family information through which an individual can seek understanding. Pastors and other church professionals will find them invaluable for reference and counseling. Though each book stands alone as a valuable resource, study materials are also provided so that they may be used in church and group settings. As a package, the Family

Concern Series offers the congregation a thorough, long-term plan for adult family-life education, and the resources for meeting the specialized family needs of its people.

The resources in the Family Concern Series focus on the needs of three audiences: single adults, never married or formerly married—married couples, with or without children —and, parents faced with child-rearing responsibilities.

Each author in this series is a committed disciple of Jesus Christ, with a concern for the local church and with a high level of expertise in his/her subject. I am pleased with the enthusiastic cooperation of all these Christian leaders.

God uses people more than books to change people, so this Family Concern Series has been designed to help people work together on their family needs. A Leader's Guide has been prepared for each book in the series. It provides a group leader thirteen, one-hour, step-by-step plans for studying together. These may be used in adult Sunday School, Sunday evening or midweek study series, small informal study groups and as seminars and workshops in conferences and retreats. These Guides include complete study plans, learning activity instructions, visual aids, and suggestions for further investigation and reading.

In addition to the Leader's Guide, a Personal Involvement Workbook accompanies each textbook. This enables each individual, whether studying in a group or alone, to get maximum benefit from the study. Each Personal Involvement Workbook includes the worksheets and activity instructions that are used in the group sessions as well as additional exercises for personal growth.

In studying each book as a group, the leader will need a Leader's Guide and each participant a Personal Involvement Workbook. Even in studying on your own or with your partner, you may want to get the Leader's Guide and start a group study yourself. Use of the Personal Involvement Workbook will increase the value of your time spent.

Since this Family Concern Series is a comprehensive resource, the needs felt by most families are included somewhere or several times in the series, even if the titles of the books do not indicate that. The chart on the following page has been prepared to help you find these specific issues in this book and in the other books in the series.

To write a "family encyclopedia" would make for dull reading, but this chart is a guide to the most important topics in each book and works as an index to the entire Family Concern Series. To find what you need, look down the alphabetical list of topics on the left side of the page. When you find what you need, follow across the page to the right, noting the asterisks (*) under the titles across the top of the page. Each book indicated deals with the subject of interest to you.

This simple device ties the whole Series together. It is a road map that can help you get exactly what you need without being encumbered with a massive and complex index or cross-reference system. It also preserves the readability of the books. This chart plus the study materials make the Family Concern Series a powerful tool for you and your church.

A special word of thanks and appreciation goes to Norman Stolpe. As Family Concern's editorial director, he served as series editor for this project. His vision and relationship with the various authors enabled the concept to take form in reality. His hard work brought the series from planning to completion.

I trust God will deeply enrich your life and family as you study and grow.

J. ALLAN PETERSEN
Family Concern, Wheaton, Ill.

GUIDE TO CURRICULUM SUBJECTS

	‡ To be published in August 1979. All others currently available.	Florio—Premarriage Two to Get Ready	Petersen—Crises	Potts—Loneliness Loneliness: Living Between the Times	Roberts—Self-esteem	Sroka—Singleness One Is a Whole Number	Wright—Communication	Johnson—Sex Education ‡	Myra—Sex in Marriage ‡	Rickerson—Fun & Togetherness ‡	Stolpe—Goals ‡	Thomason—Finances ‡	Ward—Values Development ‡
adolescent children			*		*		*	*		*	*		*
birth control		*						*	*		*		
child development					*		*	*		*			*
child discipline					*		*				*		*
child communication			*		*		*	*		*	*		*
church-family				*		*					*		*
dating		*				*			*				
death			*	*									
divorce			*	*		*							
emotions		*	*	*	*	*	*		*				
engagement		*	*						*				
finances			*									*	
friendship				*		*							
goals		*		*		*					*	*	
leisure				*		*				*	*	*	
loneliness				*		*			*				
marital communication		*	*	*					*			*	
marital conflicts		*	*						*			*	
modeling			*		*		*	*		*	*		*
role adjustment		*	*			*		*	*		*		
self-identity		*	*	*		*		*	*				
sex education		*	*					*	*				
sex in marriage		*							*				
value development								*			*		*
worship										*	*		*

1

The Joy of Trouble

As I travel, speaking to the needs of families, I meet many people concerned about the multiple crises facing families today. I also talk with people who are facing their own family crises. Everywhere I go anxious voices ask, "What is happening to our families?" Silent eyes plead, and people ask, "What can you offer my family? . . . I've got problems I haven't even used yet."

The crisis of the family is not found in sociological trends, divorce statistics, the women's movement, or changing morality. It is the accumulation of unresolved day-to-day problems in your family and mine. It is the assumption that having problems is somehow abnormal and unhealthy.

The Bible is more realistic than that. James wrote, "Consider it all joy, my brethren, when you encounter various trials, knowing that the testing of your faith produces endurance. And let endurance have its perfect result, that you may be perfect and complete, lacking in nothing" (James 1:2-4).

We've come to expect our lives to be comfortable and trouble free. When problems disrupt this pattern, we conclude that something is wrong. Whenever possible we put the blame on someone else: spouse, children, parents. Schools, society, television, even church and God become scapegoats for family crises.

James suggested that crises are opportunities for growth if they are managed with a goal in view. You can receive a crisis into your family with joy, knowing that its testing produces endurance. You can submit your family to endurance, knowing that it is necessary for maturity.

The concept of endurance is rather foreign to this technological age. We have come to expect infallible, if not instant, solutions to our problems. We become impatient when a technology can't be harnessed to solve human problems.

Families search for a formula, philosophy, method, or teacher that can insure perfect children and marital harmony. But no apparatus can generate perpetual love in a marriage. No dosage of vitamin F will preserve the faith of a teenage child. No magical adjusting of dials, levers, and switches will guarantee permanent protection from crises.

James instructed Christians to consider crisis a source of joy since they know it will cause them to grow. A positive attitude toward difficulties in the family requires a major rethinking of the meaning of trouble. The negative pattern of "How can I get this over with, as quickly and painlessly as possible?" must be replaced with, "How can I squeeze out the most growth?" The sense of isolation must be replaced with the realization that others have dealt with this crisis before.

One popular book that has highlighted the crises of adulthood is Gail Sheehy's *Passages*. While this is not a Christian's answer to her book, we do share the theme of crisis. *Passages'* definition of crisis was drawn from the work of developmental psychologist Erik Erikson and illuminates the truth of James. "Crisis 'connoted not a catastrophe, but a turning point, a crucial period of increasing vulnerability and heightened potential' " (New York: Bantam Books, 1977, p. 19).

The basis of Sheehy's book is that family crises, even of tragic proportions, can be profoundly constructive. On the other hand, even minor difficulties can be devastating for the family. The important thing is not what happens to you, but how you react to what happens.

The family has been getting a lot of attention lately, particularly in Christian circles. Much of this attention is valuable and overdue. Some of the more sensational cries, however, have given the impression that the crises of today's families are somehow unprecedented, that solutions are not available because the problems are new. Many families have been paralyzed by this fear and hopelessness. They have lost the joy of trouble to which James called all believers.

Passages is subtitled "Predictable Crises of Adult Life." A major point of the book is that all adults go through the same basic crises in some fashion. In making this assertion, the author quotes American novelist Willa Cather's observation, "There are only two or three human stories, and they go on repeating themselves as fiercely as if they had never happened before" (*Passages,* p. 28).

What is striking is not how many different crises families face but how few! They are not isolated experiences but primary threads of the fabric of human life. They are woven into each other so intimately that chapter divisions for this book can be made only arbitrarily and artificially.

The First Family

Family crises are universal. They are directly tied to the original sin of Adam and Eve. The curse that sin brought on Adam and Eve (Gen. 3:16-20) speaks of family relationships: childbearing, husbands ruling over their wives, man's toil to support his family. In the Fall, trust between husband and wife was broken.

Sin continued to have a negative impact on the family with the births of Cain and Abel (Gen. 4). In this situation the basic elements of family crises took their shape. Cain's unacceptable sacrifice implied that Adam and Eve had failed to communicate God's expectations to him. Or if they did communicate to him, he had already chosen not to fulfill God's expectations but to seek God in his own way. A breakdown in value transmission occurred between the first generation, Adam and Eve, and the second generation, Cain.

Cain's jealousy toward Abel worsened the strife and led to his killing his brother. Imagine the heartbreak of Adam and Eve when they discovered the death of Abel, who was perhaps a preferred son because of his relationship with God. With Abel dead and Cain banished, Adam and Eve were left alone.

Crisis is the inevitable outcome of sin, as shown by the first family. Adam and Eve, and Cain and Abel are representative of all families.

Other Old Testament Families

Family problems plagued many Old Testament heroes. Noah's curse (Gen. 9:20-27) set his children and their descendants against each other for generations to come. Lot struggled with his uncle Abram (Gen. 13). The contrast between Abram's approach to the crisis and Lot's is a portrait of successful and unsuccessful ways of attempting to resolve conflict. Lot never effectively dealt with the difficulties in his family. His wife turned back to die as they fled Sodom. Deterioration continued as Lot's daughters incestuously bore him sons. Nor was Abram free from family crisis. The rivalry between Hagar and Sarah, and subsequently between Ishmael and Isaac, was a source of difficulty in his household.

Isaac and Rebekah started well (Gen. 24), but slid into family crisis when they each chose a different son as their favorite (Gen. 25:28). This tragic choice, made subtly by so many parents, destroyed marital harmony to the point where Rebekah schemed with Jacob to deceive Isaac (Gen. 27:5-17). In their old age, they shared only the bitterness of Esau's pagan marriage (Gen. 26: 34-35). The story of Jacob and Esau is in many ways similar to Cain and Abel's story. Only by God's grace was this family spared fratricide (Gen. 27:41-42; 33).

Jacob, "the sneak," escaped Esau only to meet his match in Laban. In addition to in-law tensions, Jacob had to contend with the rivalries of his four wives and his children. His family deteriorated further with the sexual defiling of Dinah (Gen. 34), the covenant-breaking and adultery of Judah (Gen. 38), the death of Rachel (Gen. 35:16-19), and the disappearance of Joseph (Gen. 37).

Moses also faced trouble in his family. He argued with his wife, Zipporah, over the circumcision of their children (Ex. 4). Though Moses and his brother, Aaron, became a workteam, Aaron took over and built a golden calf while Moses received the Law (Ex. 32). Aaron and Miriam later staged a revolt against Moses' leadership (Num. 12).

Gideon's call from God placed him in conflict with his father (Judges 6). And Gideon's children, being the children of many wives, squabbled among themselves. This led to further apostasy in Israel (Judges 8:29-35). The torrid marital and sexual story of Samson created a crisis both for his parents and for the people in Israel (Jud. 13—16).

God introduced Samuel as judge, prophet and priest to replace Eli's sons. Though Eli had apparently been godly, his children did not follow in his footsteps. They caused him considerable grief and, ultimately, death. Tragically, Samuel's sons fared no better than Eli's (1 Sam. 8:1-5), which caused the people to demand a king. The stage was set for the tormented Saul. Though both Eli and Samuel had been godly men, they were grieved by wayward sons. In contrast, Jonathan, the son of disobedient Saul, was God's instrument for supporting and preserving David when Saul wanted to kill him.

The sad story continues. Though David was a man after God's heart, his family was deeply troubled by crises. David started a chain reaction in his family by not handling temptation correctly. He succumbed to adultery. Tragedy and heartbreak resulted—the murder of his army general, Uriah, the death of his child, and the waywardness of his other children.

These candid biblical accounts demonstrate that personal sin and family crisis have gone hand in hand since the earliest recording of Scripture. It is the same song—only another verse. To imagine that modern crises could be more sordid, troublesome, or distressing than those faced by these Old Testament characters is difficult indeed.

Today's Family

The family has become of great concern to our society. Thankfully, many people have been helped by this renewal. Unfortunately, the sense of urgency to do something for the family often obscures the understanding of the crises faced by families. Emphasis on extreme family problems such as child and wife abuse, incest, homosexuality, and pornography stimulate more fear than action. Focus on broad social trends such as divorce, working mothers, single parents, and family size leave one feeling helpless and hopeless. With such approaches, the "crisis of the family" can often be safely located outside *my family*.

What is the significance of these broad issues and trends for *your family and mine?* Consider the words of one observer of the family scene:

The family is going through a long and perilous crisis .

The stresses within the family and the strains from without are shaking it to its very foundations. At present, it would seem that most of the forces impinging upon the family are centrifugal ones which, gathering force and speed, are causing such a suction against its inner bonds as threatens to explode it into bits (Regina Weiman, *The Modern Family and the Church*. New York: Harper and Brothers, 1937, pp. 10, 29).

Do those words sound strangely familiar and current? They were written in 1937, which was considered a time of strength for the family. The sense of crisis in families is not new. Yet, the label "crisis" is used whenever problems no longer seem manageable.

One of the issues Christians are, and need to be, relating to is the bombardment of sexual stimuli in our culture. The advertising and entertainment industries recognize that sex is a popular moneymaker. Only a positive, biblical attitude toward sex will equip Christians to handle the problem. However, when fear escalates it to crisis proportions, even solutions are swept away by the clever bombardment of the media.

My wife heard a Christian speaker one evening and came home upset. "I got so tired," she said. "He was going on about what he called Christian pornography—blasting everything that's being written about sex." I was to have lunch with him the next day.

During lunch he turned to me and asked, "You work in the area of the family. What do you think of all this Christian pornography that's coming out now?" Not wanting to clash right away, I said, "You'll have to tell me about it—what are we talking about?" He mentioned two of the recent books by well-known Christians on sex in marriage. "Yes," I said, "I think they are fine. I've written an endorsement for each one of them." He was shocked and replied, "I would hate to have a child of mine ever happen to read any of that."

Now this is a sharp man in his early forties. But like many Christians, he doesn't know how to respond to sexual openness. It frightens and debilitates him. The questions people ask today are the ones mentioned in these books, and practical and candid answers need to be given.

My desire is to help people deal with the crises in their families by helping them to a fuller understanding of those families. We have many things to be concerned about, but in many ways, the most fundamental issues change little from one generation to the next. Part of the solution, I believe, is to look at some of the positive things that are happening to families today.

Some Positive Facts

Statistics can be dull and they are often used to paint a dark picture. Not all of them, however, are dismal. Consider some of the more encouraging facts about today's families.

The General Mills American Family Report stated that there is a mood of optimism and hope among parents. The large majority of families express satisfaction and confidence in the way they are handling their problems, the amount of fun and enjoyment they have with their children, and the way the family works together. In fact, they reported that the percentage of parents feeling this way rose from 83% in 1975 to 90% in 1977 (Yankelovich, Skelly, and White, *Raising Children in a Changing Society. The General Mills American Family Report, 1976-1977*, p. 35).

A recent study of men's attitudes toward sexuality will surprise those who thought that marriage was becoming passé. It states, "Most men *do* want to be married; over 90 percent of them." The study also reported that "since Kinsey's time there has been no increase in marital infidelity" (Anthony Pietropinto and Jacqueline Simenaur, "Beyond the Male Myth," *Ladies Home Journal,* October, 1977, pp. 125ff).

Another study compares current family statistics to those of colonial times. "Data from colonial America show that only 6 percent of U.S. households contained children, parents, and grandparents. The latest figures, for 1970, show it's still 6 percent. More families have two parents now (84.3 percent) than in colonial days (70 percent)" ("The Family's Not Dying," *National Observer,* March 5, 1977, p. 1).

Divorce statistics are frequently the villians of discouragement. They are often reported in a sensational, yet misrepresentative manner. Christian sociologist John Scanzoni of Indiana University, writes, "Approximately four out of five marriages remain intact through middle age and beyond. This means that before age 65 one out of five marriages is dissolved by either death or divorce, but not solely by the latter. . . . In fact, because of decreasing death rates, the long-range trend between 1860 and 1963 shows a steady decrease in the number of actual yearly total marital dissolutions due to *both factors combined. . . . It seems safe to conclude that more Americans are spending more years in the marital situation than ever before in our history"* (John Scanzoni, *Sexual Bargaining.* Englewood Cliffs: Prentice-Hall, 1972, pp. 11-13).

Even the preponderance of remarriage after divorce, which is a source of genuine concern to Christians, does indicate a preference for marriage and family life. On the matter of divorce, Letha and John Scanzoni update us. According to the Bureau of the Census, "about four out of every five of those who obtain a divorce will eventually remarry. . . . Evidently, men and women who decided on divorce weren't so much interested in getting out of marriage per se . . . as in getting out of a particular marriage. . . . Evidently, these second marriages are quite satisfactory to most couples involved, because divorce 'repeaters' are fewer than is sometimes assumed in popular thought" (Letha and John Scanzoni, *Men, Women, and Change.* New York: McGraw-Hill, 1976, pp. 458-459).

Despite these encouraging signs, families still face significant problems. As U.S. Vice-President Walter Mondale observed, "We can't afford any national crusades to 'save the family.' We don't need or want any new bureaucracies intruding on the privacy of family life. What we need are married couples and parents who will commit themselves to working through their crises together" (Walter Mondale, *Psychology Today.* May, 1977, p. 39).

When crises come, many prefer to run away or hide. Author Joe Bayly described this attitude: "If my wife does not help me grow, I dissolve our marriage. If I think I would find greater pleasure, perhaps the fountain of youth, in young flesh, I dissolve our marriage. If my wife has fallen behind me in intellectual growth and ability to relate to the business and social groups I aspire to—regardless of the fact that her faithfulness in providing a home and raising the children caused the gap—I dissolve our marriage.

"Or an extreme example: I heard of a man whose wife was diagnosed as having cancer. His first reaction? 'I'll divorce her' " (Joseph Bayly, "The Me Generation." *Eternity,* October 1977, p. 87).

But, running away never works. Over the years, I have seen

many people try to escape their problems by trying a new city, a new job, a new church or a new spouse, only to find that they carried their problems with them. The other pasture was not as green as they thought. Tragically, the change that was supposed to be an escape became a further snare.

There are other options than flight or fight. We can face ourselves honestly and act constructively regardless of the circumstances. We can commit ourselves to find the priceless diamond in the hard black lump of coal. But to avoid panic and collapse in a crisis, we must decide ahead of time what our response will be.

A practical formula may help—principles that can be applied to every possible crisis and can enable us to say, "God has made me fruitful in the land of my affliction" (Gen. 41:52).

2

The Action Team

Resolving family crises is a team effort with God. First, God acts on behalf of His children. Second, honest self-appraisal requires taking responsibility and acting for your own problems. These two steps cannot be separated or arranged in arbitrary priority or sequence. We must face ourselves, and we must face God.

Howard Hendricks, Christian author and lecturer, tells concerned parents that God started to work powerfully with his children when he changed his parental prayer. He had been praying, "God change my children," but changed and prayed, "God change my children's father."

Many leaders in the church have real difficulty with this. We have a ministry. We direct our energy to helping others and to supportive busywork. We feel noble and selfless. All too often, we have evaded ourselves. On the secular level, feminist Betty Friedan admitted, "It was easier for me to start the women's movement than to change my own personal life" (Gail Sheehy, *Passages,* p. 312.).

God Acts

About two-thirds of the Book of Psalms was written about how God acted in times of personal, family, and national crisis. These psalms indicate that even at the depths of doubt and despair, the acts of God are rehearsed.

Many times, a psalmist called on God, but his "soul refused to be comforted." Then, though he found no specific solution to the immediate problem, he reviewed God's acts in the past.

20

"I shall remember the deeds of the Lord; Surely I will remember Thy wonders of old. I will meditate on all Thy work, and muse on Thy deeds" (Ps. 77:11-12).

Resolving family crisis is teamwork with God. Man cannot do what only God can do. God will not do what man can do. If man takes his responsibility, God will respond with His ability. We share the responsibility to act. Active teamwork is the basis in this book for considering each of the categories of problems faced by families.

One way of understanding family crisis is to view it as an awareness of a gap between what is and what should be, the actual and the ideal. To be mature is to hold to the ideal and live with the actual. To fail is to accept the actual and totally reject the ideal. This will stimulate guilt and hopelessness.

One study points out that churches are often trapped between these two alternatives when they try to help families. "Church efforts in family education still suffer from an overdose of 'inspiration' in the program. We mean by this a tendency to instill in parents a picture of 'ideal' family life. . . . Two earmarks of this inspirational approach to family education are an idealization of family life and simplification of the problems involved . . . when it emphasizes parental responsibility, church literature . . . tends to repeat the same truisms, uses the same general statements of 'fact' as scare techniques, and give the same generalized answers to almost any family situation. Moralism runs rampant through church family literature" (Roy W. Fairchild and John Charles Wynn, *Families in the Church: A Protestant Survey*. New York: Association Press, 1961, pp. 246-247).

Let's be realistic in discussing the various kinds of family crises and avoid painting an unreal and idealized picture of the family. All families have problems and can solve them. No family is ideal, but each one can grow. No one should feel odd or guilty because he is not the perfect person, partner, or parent, or his family is not the perfect model.

Though the same basic crises come up over and over again, no two families encounter them in exactly the same way. Each family has been equipped with different experiences and resources for dealing with their difficulties. No one pattern can possibly cover all the cases for all the people for all time.

Immediate, obvious solutions are not always available. Thus, teamwork with God requires perseverance and patience. There are no instant solutions, no pushbuttons for success, no formulas for all crises or all families.

A Plan of Action
However, I do want to present a pattern of thought, a principle that will enable you to join with God to solve your family's problems.

Jesus said, "If any man is willing *to do* His will, *he shall know* of the teaching, whether it is of God" (John 7:17). Doing precedes knowing. Understanding follows action. Insight may not lead to action—but action gives insight. Our problem is usually a failure to initiate action, not a lack of sufficient information. If you genuinely desire *to do* the will of God, you may then act on the basis of what you know. Even if you do not know as exactly and as fully as you wish, you can count on God to correct your course of action and to supply more insight.

The word *act* is the key, and includes a systematic way of approaching family problems constructively.

The Act principle can be made into an acrostic for three important elements.

A—*Affirm* that God has a positive solution
C—*Commit* yourself to constructive action
T—*Trust* God for the ultimate outcome

The Act principle is more of an attitude checklist than a series of chronological steps. When faced with a problem, a couple can learn to ask: "Are we *affirming* God's plan? Are we *committed* to action? Are we *trusting* God to act?" This can become a positive and powerful habit.

Each remaining chapter in this book deals with a major family crisis. You will meet people who have faced difficulties with a unique approach, and you will see how some resolved their problems and how others failed to cope. Some followed the Act principle; others negatively bungled their way through.

Common Principles
No family crisis is unique or stands alone. It is related to every other one and in the final analysis, there are really just a few

universal problems. If you deal with every problem in isolation, what you learn from the crisis is limited and its value may not be identified. You will miss its positive effect and how it relates to the rest of life.

W. Clement Stone, who won his success in the insurance business, has said he followed this principle: after he sold something he analyzed what happened by asking, "Why did I sell those three but not the other four? What was the difference?" Then he changed his approach and went back to try and sell more. If sales did not increase, he would conduct another analysis. He kept at this till he could put into a formula what those elements of success were. Principles that worked one place would work in another.

The Act principle has been tested by experience in the same way. No matter what crisis you are facing, the Act principle will enable you to think through your relationship to God, yourself, and the situation. *Affirming* God's plan rests on a vital relationship with Him. What can you expect from Him? *Commitment* to action exposes your relationship to yourself. What is your responsibility for this crisis? *Trusting* God for the outcome assumes a proper relationship to the situation. What value can you find in this crisis?

A breakdown in any one of the levels disrupts the process. If you don't *affirm* that the problem has a solution, you will dismiss every possibility that comes your way. You will have decided it's insolvable. If you don't have a *commitment* to action, nothing will happen. You will sit passively and say, "All right, God, now what?" It's something like playing tennis with someone who never hits the ball back. *Trusting* God for the ultimate solution to the problem takes the action out of the realm of "works." You recognize that God solves the problem.

Affirmation

To *affirm* that God has a positive way of dealing with a difficulty is the first step in the Act principle. In this way, you start with God and bring His influence, providence, love, and wisdom to bear on a situation. You can then work with an attitude of thanksgiving and anticipation, even if you are not yet feeling thankful. You would not give thanks *for* the adultery which a spouse is involved in, but you can give thanks for the crisis and its potential for good. The minute you bring God into a crisis, it becomes an opportunity for both God and you. The moment you thank God, you add a dimension that moves you from being on the defensive. Instead of reacting negatively, you are free to act on the offensive.

W. Clement Stone used to say, "When I have a problem I get alone and thank God for it in these words, 'God, I thank You I have a problem. Thank You for listening to me. I ask You for direction. I don't ask You to do it for me. I ask for Your guidance. If You will tell me what to do, I will do it.' And I wait on my knees for His will and when He shows me, I get up and do it."

This affirmation also will help clarify and identify the problem by gaining God's perspective on it. With a better picture of the problem, you can identify your share in it and more easily see how to act.

Suppose your problem is simple: your first baby has been born and you're feeling uneasy and inadequate as a new father. In this case, you can probably sit down, think it through, and come to grips with your new responsibility.

But if your spouse has an affair, your emotions will be more highly charged and harder to think through. Affirming audibly that God has a plan can keep you from giving up right away. It can help clear your mind to identify underlying problems and your involvement in them. In this situation a positive, affirming step may be to seek help from your pastor, psychologist, or family counselor.

Commitment

Commitment of yourself to constructive action in your family crisis is the second step in the Act principle. Once you thank God and affirm that He has a way to deal with the crisis, you should expose yourself to finding that way.

One woman's story illustrates how a commitment to take courageous action paid off. Her husband wanted a divorce to marry a woman nearly 20 years younger than himself. After sorting through the alternatives and her emotions, she said, "I had my answer, I would sit tight; I would refuse to go along with the divorce.

"When my husband came home that night, I told him my decision and my reasoning. His being in love was undoubtedly a

THE ACTION TEAM / 25

wonderful state of being, but in degree of importance to an established home, children, and a long-standing marriage—albeit cooled down—it ranked a weak 1 on a scale of 1 to 10.

"He looked at me in disbelief and stormed out. I didn't know if he would come back or not. But he did—that evening very late. For weeks he was home only to eat and sleep. All the while, with great effort I tried to be pleasant. After all, I had insisted the marriage continue. In all fairness, I had no right to make it unpleasant, no matter how wronged I felt . . . .

"That was several years ago. Our marriage now is stronger because of its near breakup. We don't take it for granted. Both of us put forth effort to nurture a relationship that had gone stale" ("News Lady," *Chicago Daily News*, 1977).

Positive action breeds more positive action. Psychologists call it "positive reinforcement." The good feelings of progress motivate you to take further action.

Jay Adams, a pastoral counselor, tells of housewives coming to him frustrated and unfulfilled. They feel they're not getting anything done at home. He says, "Make yourself a list of things to be done and pick out one to finish this week. Go home and get your refrigerator cleaned. Next week we'll talk a little more about how you feel." So they clean the refrigerator on the first day, and they get so inspired that they do the mending too, and by the end of the week they're feeling a lot better. Constructive action motivates them to further action.

Trust

The third element in the Act principle is to *trust* God for the ultimate outcome. Trust is believing that God is too wise to make a mistake and too loving to be unkind. Trust expects results that are not necessarily simple solutions, but are best for yourself and your family.

Trusting God means not counting the score at halftime. Patience is part of faith. How many games are won in the last few minutes?

Your children may be breaking your heart and it may seem as if they never will come around, but you don't know what will happen a year from now. You can't judge any situation by its appearance today. "You have need of endurance, so that when you have done the will of God, you may receive what was promised" (Heb. 10:36).

Joseph is a classic example of a man in multiple crises following the Act principle and patiently seeing God accomplish His grand design.

The writer of Genesis states that Joseph's rivalry with his brothers led to his being sold as a slave. His refusal to sin with Potiphar's wife put him in prison, though he was innocent. He was left to languish in jail and his future looked bleak indeed.

But these crises brought Joseph the opportunity to mature beyond his bragging youth. He *affirmed* his belief in God's way and *committed* himself to right action in the worst of circumstances. He *trusted* God for the solution even when things apparently were not working out.

But God was working. "He sent Joseph as slave to Egypt to save his people from starvation. There in prison they hurt his feet with fetters, and placed his neck in an iron collar, *until God's time finally came*—how God tested his patience! Then the king sent for him and set him free. He was put in charge of all the king's possessions" (Ps. 105:17-21, LB).

"Until God's time finally came"—God was still in control during the crises. He completely reversed Joseph's fortunes. Joseph went from imprisoned slave to chief administrator of a most powerful nation—in one day! From subsisting on a prisoner's rations to being God's instrument of preservation for a whole nation in famine—in one day!

During the seemingly endless crises, God was working *in* Joseph as well as *for* him. He was changed from a pesky, bragging youngest brother to a mature, forgiving, loving protector of the very ones who betrayed him. Joseph's character was being shaped by the difficulties while God prepared him for a larger service. God chooses little people, gives them a big job, and stretches them to fit the job. We grow through crises.

3

Marriage Beginnings

They were back from their honeymoon. The living room of their small apartment was cluttered with boxes and wedding gifts. The mattress had been moved from the floor to a bedstead, and the clothes from suitcases to drawers, thanks to her parents. Chrome and formica supplanted packing crates in the kitchen, thanks to his parents. Young love was warm as they headed off to work each morning.

The direction and pace of a marriage are determined by its first weeks and months. Many choices are made—and so fast.

With the boxes out of the living room, it looked empty. An armchair, an old rocking chair, a rubber tree, and several wall plaques.

She said, "We at least need a couch and a rug. Maybe my folks would let us put something on their charge account. And I've heard some people can find good bargains at garage sales."

He said, "We'll have to start saving, I guess. It wouldn't be right to borrow from the folks. And who wants somebody else's junk? We have to do this on our own."

The first argument after the honeymoon can be a shock. What happened to the power of love that could overcome all problems? What happened to all the beautiful understanding and communication? How can history's most perfect couple not be getting along?

The early months of marriage are not usually thought of as a time of crisis. Most couples find that the thrill and excitement of all the new things plus the strength of their relationship enable them to live through these crises with a minimum of stress. No one knows before the wedding exactly what life will be like after the honeymoon. Many are caught off guard by the disagreements, difficulties, and crises that do occur. But to marry, as Christians, is a demonstration of faith in God's ability to help you grow together.

Early Marriage Crises

Divorce statistics confirm that early marriage is a time of crisis. Letha and John Scanzoni report that, "Half the divorces in the United States take place within the first seven years of marriage; and by the time fourteen years of married life have gone by, three-fourths of those couples who will become divorced have already done so" (Letha and John Scanzoni, *Men, Women, and Change,* pp. 460-461).

Newlyweds are faced with many choices soon after the wedding. The decisions they make at this time, though they may seem trivial, accumulate to form the couple's life-style together. These issues cannot all be worked through during engagement, even with the most intense premarital counseling. The faith that starts a marriage must be accompanied with commitment to continue the relationship.

Father John Powell, psychology instructor at Loyola University, recently remarked that he saw a connection between the trends of divorce and Catholic priests leaving the priesthood. He said he took his own vows for life, much as a couple pledge themselves to each other for life, and went on to observe that perhaps it is the concept of *commitment* that is passing out of vogue.

Solidifying commitment is one of the most crucial tasks of early marriage. The depth of commitment is tested when newlyweds discover their love and idealism will not protect them from disagreements and even full-scale crises.

While unexpected tragedies can descend on couples early in marriage, most of the crises during this time are those of decision-making. They are problems over which the couple has some control and power, and are not like some of the later crises which hurl people helplessly out of control. Early marriage crises are wonderful opportunities to establish constructive patterns that can be valuable when confronting the bigger crises that may strike later on.

Marriage Expectations

Each person brings his own expectations to marriage. Sooner or later, every couple comes to the realization that their expectations of marriage are not fully compatible and neither of them will have their marriage hopes completely fulfilled. Thus, the first crises of marriage are born.

The raw material for each new marriage is drawn from the marriages of the couple's parents. Many marriage expectations are unconsciously built on the years of observing the parents' marriage. Habits and patterns are established so early that they are seldom given more than a passing thought.

I often speak to college students about marriage preparations. I like to say to them, "You ought to study marriage before you think of marriage. You are probably giving more attention to the history of ancient civilization in your studies than you are to marriage. You ought to study two marriages: your own parents' marriage and the marriage of your fiancee's parents. A practical analysis of your own family background compared with that of your fiancee's will reveal how your expectations and training are likely to work out in marriage."

If you face crises early in your marriage because of differences in background, you will not be helped by reading that you should have thought of this sooner. But you can start from this point forward to deal constructively with these differences. Actually, no two people have exactly the same background and experience, so learning to deal with these differences is much more important than minimizing them.

Let's apply the Act principle to this kind of early marriage difficulty.

First, you can accept and *affirm* any differences. They are probably the things that attracted you to each other in the first place. Much of the excitement of marriage comes from the complementary fitting together of these differences. They are God's gifts to add spice to your life and help you grow. Affirm that He wants you to use these differences as important building blocks in your relationship.

In the early stages of marriage, when you may feel you are making little or no progress in adjusting to each other, *commitment* becomes vitally important. The first commitment is the one you made at your wedding, which was the basis for your formal vows. The formal wedding vows indicated your commitment was made to God, to your families, to your church, and to society, as well as to each other. Commitment is the ability to patiently stick by your promise, even when things are not working out as you had hoped.

Commitment only makes sense when you can affirm that God has a way to deal with the disappointments. It only works when you can *trust* God to reward your patience with progress.

The second commitment is to take constructive action. In some cases, this will mean sitting down together, and saying to each other, "I think we have different expectations for this. Let's try to work out a solution." For instance, you might work out the differences over resort-versus-camping vacations by using a trailer and well-equipped campground with nice facilities.

You may also need to consult outside help if a solution is not immediately apparent to you. The first choice is probably your pastor or the pastor who performed your wedding. Older married friends can sometimes help, especially if they've built a good marriage. *Seek counsel only from winners, not losers!* If the problem is serious, your best action may be to see a professional marriage counselor recommended by your pastor. Counselors can be expensive, but they are cheap compared to marital breakup and the financial loss that involves.

The Relatives

Establishing a healthy pattern of relationship with your in-laws is one of the critical tasks of early marriage. You now have two sets of parents, and often other relatives as well.

One couple started out with serious difficulties in this area, but by taking some specifically planned action, they have built solid, loving relationships with their families.

She grew up on a farm, and was part of a conservative church congregation. Her husband graduated from a progressive Christian college with a degree in philosophy. During their engagement, the son-in-law and the father-in-law often collided—the philosopher versus the farmer. Tension increased and the gap between them widened. The crisis reached its peak when they made their wedding plans The bride and groom planned their own wedding without consulting the parents, and the ceremony was not traditional, or to her parents' liking.

The son-in-law determined to develop a positive relationship with his father-in-law, but his efforts at communication seemed to backfire. He finally came to the realization that his task was to understand his father-in-law more than to get his father-in-law to understand him. Armed with that insight, he set about to learn as much as he could about the farm and farming. He asked a lot of questions and tried to be as helpful as possible whenever they visited the home place. In a remarkably short time this relationship warmed up and became quite cordial.

Without realizing it, the young man had put to work the Act principle. He *affirmed* that God had a way to a positive relationship with his father-in-law. He did not give up on that goal even though he was uncomfortable in his efforts. He *committed* himself to take some action to resolve this crisis. That action was to make himself the learner, rather than the teacher. Finally, he had to *trust* God for the results of that act of faith. He had no way of knowing how his father-in-law would respond or what change would come.

The father-in-law did respond quite positively, and they now have a very friendly relationship, but someone had to initiate the action.

Money and Housework

Money and division of labor (sometimes called sex roles) are two other areas that commonly cause trouble for newlyweds. When people discuss roles, they usually do so in theological, philosophical, and psychological terms. The questions of authority, submission, and headship are not as critical in early marriage as the practical problems of getting the chores done.

Many families have highly defined ideas of "men's work" and "women's work." While some broad categories can be laid down, many of the details cannot. For example, his father may never have taken out the garbage, and her father did it all the time. The pile of garbage in the kitchen has been the battleground for many young couples. You can probably think of your own areas of difference: scrubbing floors, gardening, washing windows, Saturday breakfast or Sunday summer cooking, cleaning up after company, and shopping. When children come, it may be feeding, changing, or picking up toys.

Both partners should ask one question when working out an agreement on specific roles: How can I best serve my partner? Serving is the essence of love, the identifying mark of the Christian and the basic element of marriage success.

The scriptural commands are, "Submit yourselves one to another in the fear of God" and "in love serve one another" (Eph. 5:21; Gal. 5:13). Committed to this principle, a couple can discuss specific tasks considering each other's needs, schedule, abilities, and desires, and work out a mutually satisfactory arrangement. Then *act* to do more than agreed on.

Expressing Sexuality

In many ways, the sexual adjustment of early marriage can be the trickiest of all. Until recently, it was not something that was talked about publicly in a helpful way. It is not uncommon for couples of all ages to be embarrassed in discussing their sexual adjustment with each other. But this should not and need not be. Following the Act principle can help you to avoid embarrassment as together you seek what God has made possible.

First, *affirm* your sexuality, and remember that God created you as a sexual person. Sex was His idea; male and female were His design. Your sexual emotions, sensations, urges, and desires are part of God's intention for your marriage. He wants you to experience a robust and hearty, tender and romantic sexuality in your relationship. Read the Song of Solomon—a chaste but candid story of wedded love. You need not be ashamed to seek these things in your sex life as a married couple. You can affirm that God has a way for you to experience the fullness of sexuality in your marriage.

Learning to adjust to each other sexually requires a *commitment* to several definitive actions. Perhaps most important is to start talking to each other about your sexual expectations and questions. Discovering each other's sexual nature can be one of the greatest delights of early marriage. I frequently tell audiences that we should not be ashamed to consider what God was not ashamed to create.

Christian young couples who have been sheltered or reserved

about sexual things may find this particularly difficult to start. You can, however, commit yourselves to reveal yourselves to each other, verbally as well as nonverbally, and *trust* God to honor that with greater sexual satisfaction for both of you. If talking together about your sexuality continues to be a problem for one or both of you, seek some outside help. One very healthy commitment to action is to agree to read some books together. A number of good ones are available, written from medical and biblical perspectives, and an alert pastor or counselor can help you get started.

Innocence is one thing, but ignorance is entirely different. Christian couples rightly want to bring sexual innocence to marriage, but that is no excuse for damaging the sexual experience of marriage with continued ignorance.

Commitment in sexual adjustment demands patience. Sexual fulfillment is learned—learning how to satisfy the other, to be unselfish, self-controlled, and lovable. Some of the best things about sex simply require practice. Impatience with performance will only spoil the results. So take delight in what you are experiencing and don't give up learning. Pleasure does not require perfection!

Birth Control and Children

Sex makes babies, so an important part of sexual adjustment early in marriage is coming to a mutually agreeable approach to birth control and having children.

The Bible says much about sex, the role of partners, parental responsibilities, and morality, but nothing on the matter of birth control. Nowhere does the Bible indicate that every man and woman must be married and assume the responsibility of parenthood, nor does it teach that sex in marriage is only for procreation and every interference with this is sinful. But, the psalmist states graphically, "Children are a gift from God; they are His reward. Children born to a young man are like sharp arrows to defend him. Happy is the man who has his quiver full of them" (Ps. 127:4-5).

Over and over again the Bible tells of couples who desired children, prayed for them, and greatly rejoiced over them. What parent has not learned that children satisfy a normal desire, bring deep joy, and help the parents themselves to grow and mature.

The presence of children opens a new world to a couple and can be a means of bringing them closer together and discovering a fulfillment found in no other way. The matter of a family should be frankly discussed before marriage.

However, the Bible does not say how many children a family is to have. This would be impossible. The families in the Bible were not all the same size. The number of children in each family followed no set pattern. Each family situation is different, and each has its own resources and problems. The consideration of one family may not apply to another, and each must find God's desire and will in their personal situation.

God holds parents responsible for each child they have. Parenthood is a total responsibility, not just a biological process. We are responsible for a child's well-being and development, his spiritual growth and nurture, and his mental and social maturity. Having children is more than just giving birth to them. It is possible to sin against children already born by having others, and the preservation and maturing of life already in existence take precedence over a life that does not exist. It is irresponsible for a couple to bring more children into the world than they can nurture spiritually, financially, emotionally, and educationally.

A couple's approach can fit in with the Act principle. Each partner *affirms* that God has a plan for them as a couple, that He has the answer to a present decision and their future well-being. They *commit* themselves to the action of knowing what the Bible teaches, and of careful thought and discussion with each other. They *trust* God to provide them with the insight they need to make a decision in a time appropriate to their best long-range interests. How and what they decide will, in many ways, determine the future of their marriage.

Church Involvement

I have left until last what is perhaps the most important question for newlyweds to answer. What will their pattern of church participation be? Answering this question can be either the source of more difficulty or a means of resolving many of the other crises. I recognize that many young people are disappointed in the church today and are choosing not to participate in church life.

Solid church relationships, however, are a shock absorber for marital and family crises. When a congregation is operating as the New Testament indicates the church should, it will be a network of people who care deeply about each other. It will be a kind of spiritual extended family. You will be able to see how other couples and families work. Strong friendships will enrich your marriage and family. When crises come, and they will, you will have Christian brothers and sisters ready to cry and pray with you. Some with special gifts will be available for counsel and advice. You will see that other people face similar problems and find God's way to meet their needs. The church family will become God's support team for your family in practical and real ways. If you do not have such a church in your community, you and several couples could begin this kind of a caring fellowship within the church.

The church can also provide for you the opportunity to serve other people. God has given you unique gifts, abilities, experiences, and insights that are just what someone else needs in their crisis. Knowing that you are really helping someone else can be the reinforcement you need to conquer your problems. Serving others can be the source of energy and confidence you need to get your marriage vigorously rolling. Like our Lord, we are not here to be served but to serve, and to give our lives to set others free.

Depending on the experiences you have had, relating to a congregation may be an act of faith. If you have had a series of hurts and disappointments, you may have a hard time overcoming your fears. If you have not grown up with active church participation, you may not know how to get started.

You will have to *affirm* that God wants every believer, including you, to be intimately related to a local church fellowship. Affirm that the church is God's chosen avenue for building believers and working in the world. Affirm that God has a place in the church for you.

Commitment by a young couple to a local church may require considerable courage. The trends among your peers are against it. If you are in a new locality, seek a church that loves the Bible and with which you can be involved to the maximum. Avoid the congregations that let you slip in and slip out unnoticed. Find other young couples who know Jesus Christ and with whom you can share the experiences of early marriage. Establish warm relationships with older people who have built radiant marriages. Participate in congregational polity and decision-making processes as much as possible. With these kinds of solid actions, commit yourselves to a specific congregation intentionally. "Church hopping" can only disrupt the relationships needed for your own growth and for serving.

You can *trust* God to use the church as an aid to your personal and marital growth. You can trust Him to give you opportunities for service and influence in the church And, if the church is not all it should be, you can trust God to change the church.

Because of the importance of the church in the life of every believer, young couples who are serious about their Christian discipleship and the quality of their marriage will make the effort to establish solid relationships in a local fellowship. If you disagree on the selection of a congregation, work through that to make a mutual commitment. Deal with your differences in church background and taste just as you would any other difference in your marriage. Trust God to use His people to help you grow together.

4

And Baby Makes Three

A woman wrote for help: "When I first learned for certain I was pregnant, I was unbelievably happy. But as the months have gone by, I've become awfully listless and blue. And I'm shamefully short-tempered. I know I must be terribly difficult to live with . . . I realize I'm going through a lot of physical changes right now too. I know that certain muscles are under more of a strain . . . every pregnant woman I've talked to complains about being tired. It's a natural thing. After all, I can't sleep in some of the positions I used to find restful, and baby seems to be taking trampoline lessons almost every night at bedtime . . . There is still some fear of the unknown. After all, it will make a big difference in our lives. And maybe, no matter how much I'm looking forward to the baby, I'm not exactly looking forward to all those schedule disruptions and diapers and middle-of-the-night feedings . . . I feel pretty foolish writing to you like this. I'm afraid I'm making some gigantic problem out of nothing. When I sit down to analyze it, I can think of all kinds of reasons why I'm feeling so awful, but I can't seem to convince myself that the answers I'm coming up with are an adequate explanation for the way I feel" (Lillian Kemper and Andrea Herman, "What About Those Pre-Baby Blues?" *Marriage and Family Living,* September, 1977, pp. 13-15).

This woman has identified a number of the common areas in which the birth of a child becomes a crisis, whether it is the first or the tenth. The popular expectations of joy over the birth of a child often mask the sense of uneasiness that lies just below the surface for the couple. Part of the answer given to this woman's letter recognizes this reality.

"The picture of the happy, healthy, radiant expectant mother is such a common fantasy that everyone has come to expect it, even pregnant women themselves. So when the anticipated 'glow' fails to set in, it's natural to wonder why and to cast about rather frantically for reasons" (Kemper and Herman, "What About Those Pre-Baby Blues?" p. 15).

Once the common crises associated with pregnancy and birth are recognized as normal, they can be dealt with more easily. A birth brings many profound changes to a couple and their families, and requires a flood of fresh decisions. The upheaval of change and the pressure of decision-making is a source of crisis.

A more complete understanding of what is happening, particularly with the first child, can minimize the trauma. Other situations add a unique dimension to pregnancy and birth, and we will discuss these later in the chapter.

The Process of Birth

Birth is not an instant event. Couples usually proceed toward it gradually. When a couple first decides to have a baby, their sexual lovemaking takes on a new meaning. The question, "Will this be the time?" is felt if not spoken. Marital frequency and expectations of performance may change markedly once the decision has been made.

After a few months of waiting and wondering, perhaps with mild disappointment, the preliminary announcement is made. "I think I'm pregnant. I'll see the doctor next month." Announcements to close friends and family follow the doctor's confirmation, and then the rapid physical changes which make further announcements necessary.

During this time, many changes take place in the woman. Understanding and enjoyment of the time of waiting can result from reading materials that describe the changes a step at a time. Both husband and wife need this understanding. Ask your doctor to suggest helpful literature.

The Act principle can help you handle the changes brought by pregnancy. *Affirm* that birth is a normal and natural part of life. Recognize that these things have been faced by every generation for thousands of years. *Commit* yourselves to get more information, if that is what you need. Read, talk with people you know who have had positive birth experiences, and avoid scare stories from well-meaning but uninformed people. Be ready to make some changes in your life-style. By talking out a few minor adjustments, you may be able to prevent considerable difficulty. Finally, relax, and *trust* God to bring you through these changes so that you will be better off than you were when you started. Enjoy the experience. Particularly with smaller families today, pregnancy and birth are experiences you may have only a couple of times in your life. Make the most of them!

Decisions

A host of decisions must be made before the birth of a child. With a first child, the number of decisions can be overwhelming. Some are routine, such as decor and equipment for a nursery, and picking names. They are usually the source of excitement and heighten the anticipation of the good things about the arrival of the child. If your relationship is strained at this time, however, even these things can become a battleground.

A number of other decisions are of more consequence and need to be made carefully by a couple. They are controversial issues, and your decision may subject you to some criticism from others. What kind of birth method will you use? Conventional or natural? Some doctors specialize in the care of couples who want their babies born at home. Your selection of doctor and desired approach to childbearing will have to be coordinated.

Is Father to be present for the delivery? Many hospitals allow and encourage this practice. More often than not Father is the one reluctant to take part. Very few fathers, however, who have witnessed the births of their children regret their participation.

Will you nurse or bottle-feed your baby? For a long time the technological thrust of our culture encouraged bottle feeding. But the emphasis on the natural in the last few years has somewhat reversed that trend. Nursing in public is still taboo in most circles, but discretion, planning, and practice can reduce that as a hindrance.

You may be pressured by friends and family to decide these questions in a certain way. The nature of the pressure and the degree to which you are informed may determine if these issues become a crisis in your relationship. *Affirm* that God has a plan for the birth of your child that is right for you. *Commit* yourselves to make an intelligent decision. Study these choices and talk them out together. A husband's support can make all the difference to a wife if she is under pressure. Once you make a decision, don't be pulled back into uncertainty unless you are really convinced that you did not make your first decision properly. Then *trust* God for a delightful experience. Use the time of pregnancy and birth to grow closer to each other by sharing the experience as fully as possible.

And the Grandparents

Parents can apply considerable pressure when you are pregnant, especially if this is your first child. They may be unaware of changes in medical practice in the last 30 years. They may have prejudices and misinformation which you will have to listen to and tactfully work around. They may even intrude on your decisions about nursery decor and names.

One couple was living across the country from the husband's parents when both of their children were born. During the pregnancies, his father would phone and try to talk them into naming the baby after him. Ironically, both the children were born on his birthday, and the parents were grateful that they were girls and did not have to be named after Grandpa.

When these conflicts arise, *affirm* that this is your child and your family. *Commit* yourselves to making your own decisions, intelligently and mutually. Also commit yourselves to listen politely, even if you don't always accept the advice. Finally, *trust* God to build your relationship with your parents. Even if it seems impossible now, parents will cooperate with your plans to have your children as your own.

The success of one couple is reported by Muriel Shapp, wife of Pennsylvania Governor Milton Shapp.

"Once Lucy enlists Will's muscle, the baby's room begins to resemble a tent, its red-striped baseboard mimicking the curbing of a circus ring and menagerie inhabiting the wallpaper. A minor miracle occurs. She pleasantly vetoes her mother's insistence on pale green gingham, and Will helps her resist his mother's not so subtle offers to stake them to French Provincial baby furniture. A major miracle occurs. Somehow both mothers survive the rebuffs without being permanently crushed, and everyone is on the way toward an appreciation of how comfortable it is not to have to control or struggle against attempts at control, however benevolent they seem" (Muriel Shapp, "Couples Becoming Families." *Marriage and Family Living,* October 1977, p. 10).

Pregnancy and the birth of a child will alter your marriage relationship. This is nowhere more evident than with sex. As her pregnancy progresses, the wife may feel unattractive and awkward. Certain sexual practices that were pleasant before may become uncomfortable especially in the later months. Many husbands find their swelling wives increasingly stimulating, perhaps because that is evidence of their sexual potency. Others find that their sexual fervor for their wives declines.

Most doctors recommend a period of sexual abstinence immediately before and after the birth of the child. This can add stress to the marital relationship in an already difficult time. Many books about sexual relationships in marriage offer suggestions to couples on sex during pregnancy. Information mixed with understanding and patience will smooth out this difficult time in a marriage.

Now That the Baby Is Here

Handling responsibilities after the baby arrives can also cause trouble. The sooner you agree on, and start using, your own approach to child-rearing, the easier it will be for you and the child. Men are being encouraged to take a more active role in child-rearing than was true a generation ago. Feminists want fathers to share equally in the responsibilities for the child they started. This is a good idea. Traditionalists want father to take the lead in determining child-rearing practices. This seems wise.

In her article, Muriel Shapp tells of the stress a father of twins created by not taking a fair load of work with the babies. "Seemingly unaware of bathinettes, cribs, infant seats, and plastic panties, he rejoins his TV, leaving Polly to juggle boys, diapers, baths, feedings, and housework. She wearily complains to a mate who is master of selective deafness" (Muriel Shapp, "Couples Becoming Families," p. 11).

I can't bypass this opportunity to say something about father-ing. In recent years, a number of books have been written to fathers by Christian and secular authors. The importance of a father's contribution to his children is getting more attention than ever before. I am excited about this trend and wish I had had this help when I was a new father. For too long we men have fathered children and left them for our wives to raise. We've jumped in only when extraordinary discipline was needed or for those spe-cial "manly" outings, such as the annual fishing or hunting trip.

Men, our children need us. They need our tenderness and strength. Emotionally, they need our eye contact, focused atten-tion, and laughter. Physically, they need our play and touching. Spiritually, they need to hear us talk freely about our faith in Christ. They need to see us love our wives with unembarrassed affection. They need times of intimate conversation, learning about our jobs, and discussing their own special concerns.

Parental Responsibility

Sometime between the words, "I think I'm pregnant" and "It's a girl," comes the realization of a new responsibility. It is more awesome than anyone can comprehend. The Bible does not tell each couple how many children they should have but it does state that we are totally responsible for each one we do have. The first child introduces you to the most dramatic and crisis-prone change in your life. But you can get ready, and the Act principle can help.

The Bible repeatedly *affirms* that children are gifts from God. (See Gen. 48:9; Ps. 127:3-5.) Even in adverse circumstances, you can affirm that your child is God's gift. No matter how in-adequate you feel about responsibilities of parenthood, you can affirm that God will give you the ability to rear just as He has given you the ability to bear.

This calls for a *commitment* to action. You can say, "I am a parent. I can and will act like a parent. I will be responsible for this child. I will read everything I can and increase my knowl-edge and ability." This chapter has already referred to many of the kinds of actions that need to be taken as the birth of the first child approaches. You should also consciously commit the child to God and seek God's plan for him. Infant dedication is a public and formal way to make this commitment. Then you will have to *trust* God to provide the guidance, wisdom, and ability He has promised (James 1:5-6).

Unique challenges come with the birth of subsequent children. Most important is preparing the older child or children. This starts even before pregnancy. If your conversation includes the possibility of more children with a sense of positive anticipation, the announcement of a coming sister or brother will be received with more excitement.

When you know another one is on the way, the children should be included in your joy and planning as soon as possible. They may even be told to keep this a special secret. Talk frequently and *honestly*—the new baby will not immediately be someone they can play with. Try to see this as your child does. Patiently answer questions and listen to concerns and anxieties without judgment.

You will need to replenish your nursery, and make arrangements for the older children's care while Mother is in the hospital. By all means, Father, be sure your wife comes home to a clean, organized, well-stocked house. Get help if you need it. Nothing spoils the fun of the new baby as fast as unmade beds, dirty dishes, piles of laundry, and squabbling, tired children to greet her on arrival.

Early Pregnancy

Everything in this chapter has been quite normal and predictable. All parents experience crises in some form or another. Unfortunately, not all births go smoothly. Many couples are plunged into serious crisis by a pregnancy too soon or too late. For others, childlessness is the problem. A birth can be the occasion for deep human tragedy.

Any college or seminary professor can tell of students whose educational plans were rocked by the birth of a child. Some couples, with adequate financing and determination, can complete their education. For others, it is the end of education. Either way, the emotional trauma can be considerable. Money is tight; living space is limited; the couple may be far from home, friends, relatives, and familiar surroundings. They may feel they have nowhere to turn. The wife may be especially lonely, and resentment will grow toward the husband who has the opportunity, through classroom work, to spend time with other adults and enjoy the stimulation of his studies. He may even devote himself so fully to his studies that he does not get involved in child-related chores. If the wife feels this is a cop-out on his part, the problem is compounded.

One couple found themselves pregnant almost immediately following their wedding. The wife still had nearly a year of college to complete. The husband was working on a graduate degree. They never had an opportunity to find out what life would be like for just the two of them, because the impending birth of their child dominated their thinking. How were they going to manage once the baby was born? The wife struggled through in the cramped quarters of their tiny apartment. Neither of them really wanted a baby at that time, and the child felt that rejection during his growing years.

Despite the difficulties, they persisted in their commitment to finish school and raise their family. Almost 20 years later, their children have grown to be basically healthy individuals well on their way to establishing their own lives. The parents have each completed advanced degrees, they have had rewarding professional careers and as their children approach adulthood, they are anticipating the companionship of coupleness they were not able to have as newlyweds.

Unplanned pregnancy can be a trauma, whether it happens before the wedding or when the youngest child is almost grown. Finding God's way in these situations is not easy, and this will be considered in chapter 10.

For other couples, the crisis is the inability to get pregnant. The biblical accounts of Sarah, Rebekah, Rachel, Hannah, and Elizabeth tell the poignant disappointment of not having children. Though modern culture does not attach shame to infertility as the ancients did, it can still be a serious crisis.

The pressure of potential grandparents (and often their friends) for children is hard enough for the couple who is simply delaying childbearing until it is wise. Those who are voluntarily childless may be seriously criticized if they make their decision known. But such pressure can be devastating for the couple who is trying everything in an unsuccessful attempt to get pregnant.

Prayer and Friends

Consider how the prayers of supportive friends helped one couple resolve their crisis. They wanted children very badly but it seemed impossible. Visits to their family physician and a fertility clinic brought no success. They shared their frustration and disappointment with friends in their Bible study group. The group agreed that praying together for a child for this couple was an appropriate act of faith, and waited eagerly for news that the wife had become pregnant. After a number of months of waiting, the couple considered adoption, but were daunted by the long waiting list at the agencies.

To their great delight, however, in a few months a child was available for adoption. Two years later they were able to adopt another child. So while the prayers of the friends had been made with the expectation of a natural birth, God answered the need of this couple through two adopted children who would ordinarily not have been available to them. Their parents' apprehensions and subtle criticism evaporated as they fell in love with their new grandchildren.

For other couples, pregnancy and birth are human tragedies. Though modern medicine has sharply reduced the incidence of infant and mother mortality, certain kinds of birth defects, and brain damage, they still occur. Crises of this nature are never fully resolved and are not easily dealt with. The process of healing and growth goes on for years. Some spend the rest of their lives angry at God for their tragedy.

One noticeable contrast is a professor and his wife at a well-known Christian college, who raised their children successfully to the teen years. The wife then discovered she was pregnant. Despite good medical care, the baby was born with Downs Syndrome and was seriously mentally handicapped. This couple chose to raise and care for their child in their own home. For the first few years, the older children helped, but they grew up and moved out on their own.

With tears, prayer, and courage, the couple shared their lives and selves with their child. The bittersweet joys of that experience were shared with the students at the college. This couple did much more than provide adequate care for their child by their positive approach. They were a living lesson to thousands of students of patience and love, of human dignity and God's value on even seemingly lowly people. They were living proof that God is able to meet the needs of His people in any extremity.

5

The Best Reasons Are the Little Ones

A recent series of television commercials portrays the magical power hamburgers and french fries have on children. Tears are dried, hurts vanish, disappointments are forgotten at the mere suggestion of a french fry. The final appeal to parents is to make their children happy. After all, "the best reasons for going to McDonald's are the little ones."

The arrival of that first "little one" is often the most dramatic change that ever occurs in either the life of an individual or the relationship of a couple. The parent-child relationship is perhaps the most crisis prone of all human relationships. A number of books have been written on how to raise your children, but they have not reduced this tendency toward crisis.

The point of this book is not to make crises go away. That would be impossible and probably unhealthy anyway. But you can learn to act constructively when you are faced with times of crisis.

Priorities

Dr. James Dobson, author of books on child-rearing, has said, "There's a tremendous amount of guilt involved in raising a family today." In that same interview, he was asked, "What do you consider to be the most serious interferences with meaningful family life today?" To which he answered, "Fatigue and time pressure . . . I call this condition 'routine panic.' "

How true. Everywhere I go, I meet parents who are overcommitted. Fathers are especially vulnerable. Even Christians have been fooled into believing that personal worth depends on economic success.

Dr. Dobson mentioned that he once chose family over work. "I had reserved the entire weekend to spend with my wife and children, but an emergency came up and I was unable to be at home. I had begun to fall back into the old habit of overwork that I've tried to conquer. So Sunday night I called my secretary and told her I would not be in on Monday and asked her to clear my calendar.

"The next morning, my wife Shirley and I left in the car—I didn't even tell her where we were going—and we drove to the loneliest beach we could find. We sat down on a large rock surrounded with our Bibles and had devotions. We discussed our calendar and talked about where we were going, and consciously 'listened' to each other. We then walked four or five miles up and down the beach and spent the rest of the day poking in and out of little shops and walking holding hands. I think it was one of the most enjoyable and restful days of my life. Of course, I paid a penalty for not working that day, and some of the things I was supposed to accomplish are still on my desk. But I had to decide what really mattered, and from that perspective, my family should always come first" (James Dobson, *Eternity,* October 1977, p. 84).

This crisis of insufficient time for the family disrupts the important interaction that must occur between children and their parents if the children are to learn how to be adults. Urie Bronfenbrenner, professor of human development and psychology at Cornell University, notes, "The child should spend a substantial amount of time with somebody who's crazy about him. . . . There has to be at least one person who has an irrational involvement with that child, someone who thinks that kid is more important than other people's kids, someone who's in love with him and whom he loves in return. . . . One really isn't enough . . . Let me lay out the ideal situation as I see it. It's good for a child to be in the company of people who are crazy about him for a substantial number of hours every day. I'm sure of that. But it is also good to be with people who are not crazy about him"

(Urie Bronfenbrenner, "The Erosion of the American Family," *Psychology Today,* May 1977, p. 43).

A commitment of your time to your children is the first essential element to providing this kind of relationship for them. But I think we have another crisis for our children of almost equal proportions. Our society is structured to separate adults from children and even children from each other according to their ages. This pattern pervades school, community, entertainment, and even church.

Intergenerational Relationships

In that same interview, Dr. Bronfenbrenner talked about the dangers he sees in what he has called "age segregation." "We need to make it possible for children and adults to enter each other's worlds. It will be good for both of them" ("The Erosion of the American Family," p. 45). He points an accusing finger at the junior high school as the institution that most blatantly reflects this trend.

"You can get competent, able, compassionate kids coming into that system, and junior high can turn them into kids out of *Lord of the Flies* [by William Golding]. Junior high isn't just segregated from different ages but from almost everything about society. . . . Junior high is one of the most isolated institutions we have and that's dangerous" ("The Erosion of the American Family," p. 46).

Churches too are guilty. In the past 30 years, churches have created an increasing number of age-segregated Christian education programs. Each one has its good intentions, but the total result may have hindered the development of loving, caring relationships that children need with adults. Unfortunately, as many churches have sensed that their families need help, they have added on still more programs, which only increase the time crisis. For too many children, the church is a place of isolation.

You can, however, act on behalf of your children. First, set aside time when you can devote your attention to them. Small doses every day, larger blocks of time on a regular basis, and significant specials occasionally. Author and speaker Charlie Shedd suggests a weekly date with each child. The child knows Father is at his disposal for that block of time, and the child usually chooses the activity they will share. Develop a plan that fits your family.

Second, arrange for your children to become friends with other adults. Commit your family to using hospitality to bring adults and children of different ages into the lives of your children. A few of these people will "click" with your children and become special to them for the rest of their lives.

One young family I know has occasionally invited single young adults to stay with them for a few months while they were in transition from one stage of life to another. A few have been students who had no plans for summer vacation. One was a missionary couple's daughter waiting for her parents to return on furlough. Another was a secretary for a mission board who needed a place to live while she found a roommate and apartment.

The children in this family, not to mention the parents, have been deeply enriched by these experiences. They have learned about other parts of the country and the world. They have learned consideration and respect for the needs and privacy of others. They have shared in both the troubles and joys of people at a different stage of life than their parents. They have observed people taking a variety of approaches to seriously pursuing their Christian discipleship. Perhaps most important, they have given and received love with a few other people.

You do not need to turn your home into a boardinghouse, but make it a point frequently to have dinner guests. And even though it might seem easier, don't always separate the children from the adults for eating. The risk to the dining room carpet is small compared to the benefit your children will receive from having adult friends.

Your church is the primary source for people with whom your family can have long-standing relationships. But don't stop there. Include traveling missionaries, singles, students, families with children, and older couples. You and your children may even have angels among your friends if you are hospitable in this way (Heb. 13:2).

Crisis of Adolescence
What parent has not heard of and feared the crisis of adolescence? I cannot give you an infallible formula for getting through this

period without problems. No one can. Parenthood comes with no guarantees. However, it can be said that *what you fear is likely to come upon you.* One couple assumed their sons would rebel and break away during the teen years. As they approached this age, they applied more and more restrictions with the hope of holding on to them as long as possible. Now the boys are in high school and the parents have lost control of them.

Dr. Albert Bandura, psychologist and former president of the American Psychological Association, did a thorough study on adolescents and their parents from a secular perspective. His conclusions offer some practical and hopeful insights for Christian parents of teens.

Myths of Adolescence

Dr. Bandura argues that the "storm and stress" view of adolescence is a myth and that "the stresses of the adolescents are largely products of difficulties begun in preadolescent social experiences."

He reports that research indicates that by the time young people reached adolescence, "they had internalized their parents' values and standards of behavior to a large degree." Therefore, the young people "did not regard their parents or other authority figures as adversaries, but more as supportive and guiding influences." Parents of adolescents will be more effective when they behave as "supportive, guiding influences" rather than behaving as adversaries with an "us vs. them" view of their children.

One of the classic descriptions of adolescence is that young people are fighting to gain independence from their parents. Dr. Bandura argues that "emancipation from parents has been more or less completed rather than initiated at adolescence." This suggests that parents should focus on the preteen years as a time of building a sense of personal responsibility and independence in their children so they can increasingly let go, allowing teens to be their own persons.

Another classic myth of adolescence is that of competition between the influence of parents and the influence of the peer group. On the basis of accumulated data, Bandura argues instead that "adolescents tended to choose friends who shared similar value systems and behavioral norms" with their parents. "Membership in the peer group did not generate familial conflicts. In fact, the peer group often served to reinforce and uphold the parental norms and standards of behavior" (Albert Bandura, "The Stormy Decade: Fact or Fiction?" *Power Psychology in the Schools,* 1964, pp. 224-231).

Bandura's findings point strongly to the importance of the church and church participation for the whole family during the preadolescent years, so young people will have a range of available friends who share common values with parents. An open home policy would be an extension of the church and allow young people to invite their friends home frequently and help them feel welcome there.

Parents often unwittingly encourage a "self-fulfilling prophecy." If they are expecting positive and rewarding relationships with their preadolescent children, they are, nevertheless, bracing themselves for the stormy adolescent period. Such vigilance can very easily create a small turbulence itself. When the prophesied storm fails to materialize, many parents begin to entertain doubts about the normalcy of their youngster's social development.

Do not be unduly apprehensive about the approach of adolescence. This negative sense of anticipation, more than anything else, can bring on teenage rebellion. Just at a time young people are ready to be more responsible, stand more on their own, have greater personal freedoms, be trusted more by their parents, and be better able to handle their own maturity, parents clamp down out of fear of this approaching adolescent storm, in exactly these areas, stifling what should be a very positive stage of development.

Television

If any one device symbolizes the crises of modern parent-child relationships, it is television. The way television is used in most homes is destructive of the time parents and children have together and serves to isolate them further from each other. I believe you can act to make television a powerful tool to help your children. But it will require a great deal of discipline.

Start positively by affirming that television can be used constructively in your home. *Affirm* that God has a way for you to put television to work in building relationships with your children and providing time together. *Commit* yourselves to a plan of controlled, purposeful family television viewing. *Trust* God to help

you through the hassles that will occur when you start on the plan
to a more rewarding family life.

One family with teenage children has set two standards for
television viewing. First, each person is limited to one program
per day. Second, the choices come from an agreed-upon list of
acceptable programs. At the beginning of the season, the family
looks over the new programs and selects those they think they
might want to watch during the year. They watch these together.
Then they discuss the programs and decide if they should be on the
approved list. While the parents have final say, they are usually
able to point out the problems with objectionable programs so
that their children reject them on their own.

A plan like this helps keep television under control. One
church has even gone a step further on occasion. Certain special
programs offer the family unique opportunities for discussion of
important questions. This one congregation has sometimes prepared viewing and discussion guides for families to use. When
Fiddler on the Roof was shown, they had a shortened evening
service to explain how to use a discussion guide. The families
with color television invited others into their homes to view the
program with them. Even if your church does not formally promote such shared viewing experiences, you can select certain
quality programs and invite others to view and discuss them with
your family.

The crisis that television brings to the family is its inescap-
ability. Though many families would profit from not having a set,
even that will not eliminate its influence. It must be controlled
and used constructively. You cannot prevent your children from
knowing about the sub-Christian standards reflected in television,
because they are the standards of the world around you. But you
can teach your children discernment and help them sort out the
helpful from the degrading.

Television often becomes a substitute for family reading. Children who cannot read for personal enjoyment are impoverished.
Mere reading skills are not enough; parents have to act to set a
pattern of reading in the home. Reading aloud together as a family should be a regular practice from the time the first little one
is born until the last big one leaves home. Family reading is
probably the most positive alternative to the crisis of television.

Growing Pains

Perhaps as you read about time, relationships, and television, you are thinking, "These are not the crises that break parents' hearts. What about rebellious teenagers, drugs, sex, and school dropouts?" These acute problems usually find their roots in the more common chronic situations of time, relationships, and television.

In the limited space of this chapter, I couldn't possibly write about all of the crises parents face with their children. So I have tried to lay a foundation for action in the areas where the problems start. I also want to offer you encouragement.

Children, teenagers, and young adults are still in the process of growing. This particular crisis may be a necessary step to maturity. You do not know what the years will bring in the life of your child. Trusting your child to God and waiting may severely tax your faith, but it is also the most important thing you can do as a parent.

One young couple broke their parents' hearts with the way they started life together. The parents were ready to give up and count this as the final score. But God was working.

They had both been raised in stern homes. The young man's parents were Christians but his wife's were not. They both rebelled against the strictness and shared a revolt against their upbringing. Prior to marriage, they had joined the counterculture rebellion, plunged into sex and drugs, and forgotten their family responsibilities.

After many months of marriage, each of them did some private thinking. The young woman felt some need for a relationship with God. The young man was gaining an increased appreciation for the church in which he had grown up and his friends there. He began attending church and renewed his commitment to Christ. The church fellowship accepted his wife, and the young woman became a Christian.

Patterns set during the early months of their marriage continue to plague them. He occasionally rebels against the structures and expectations of the church and drops out, sometimes for months at a time. She has grown as a Christian and is in more active fellowship with the whole body than her husband. Periodically, this erupts into tension between them.

During some of their best times they are quite involved in spiritual things, in very helpful and wholesome ways. During the worst of their times, they are sullen and uncommunicative without regular contact with the fellowship. Though they are still struggling with their own spirituality, their past history indicates that God is at work in their lives and can be trusted to complete what He has started in them (Phil. 1:6).

Problem Preparation

Childhood is growth, and growth brings crisis. Parents can prepare themselves and their children for some of the difficulties that inevitably accompany childhood.

A magazine article, "Preparing Children for Change" suggests a strategy for preparing for some of the most common crises of childhood. While some of these problems may seem trivial to adults, they can be monumental to a small child. This advice is so practical, I wanted to give it to you just as it appeared in the magazine.

> The child who has been shown the way to school before the first day, who knows what to expect when he goes to the eye doctor, the youngster who has seen the anesthesiologist's mask before surgery—these children will have fewer fears, more confidence. . . . You can let your youngster watch your teeth being cleaned, say, before he himself goes to the dentist. When you're about to visit adult friends, you can help prepare your child by bringing along some books and toys.
>
> Talking helps, too. We sometimes play a dinner table game called, "What if?"
>
> What if there were a car pool mix-up and a child wasn't picked up from an outing. What would you do? The first time we brought this up, our oldest child immediately suggested calling home, from a pay phone if necessary.
>
> "But I don't know how to use a pay phone," protested Betsy, our youngest.
>
> We hadn't realized that, so after dinner my husband took Betsy down to the gas station where she could practice dialing and putting in her dime. Sometime later when Betsy did get left at the community center by mistake, she

didn't panic. She just took the emergency dime we had provided her with, and called home.

We've discussed more serious possibilities too—home fires, approaches by strangers, accidents and injuries. Knowledge is a form of protection, and "What if" stockpiles it ("Preparing Children for Change," *Parents' Magazine,* June 1976, p. 31).

Sex Education

Teaching children about sex is one of the more serious crises shared by all parents. Probably only a small portion of all parents give any practical sex education to their children. The seriousness of this neglect is compounded because of the sex saturation of our society. The church should not only train parents to do this, but should have a program of graded sex education for all its people. A wholesome and candid sex education is conducive to a life of purity in our children and teens. A parent must feel good about his own sexuality or he will never be able to impart the right attitudes to his family.

Parents' own experiences and backgrounds often inhibit them from providing their children with the adequate sex education they need. But this need not be an obstacle to taking constructive action in this area.

One father confessed that as a child he received very little information about sex. Masturbation became a problem when he entered puberty. Guilt feelings resulted, and were catastrophic for him, particularly since he was a pastor's son.

As an older teen, he frequently found his dating practices were planned to manipulate girls for his own sexual gratification through fantasy. Of course, these fantasies further fed his difficulties with masturbation.

With this background, he has a hard time being open with his children about sex, even though he really wants to be. He feels that he failed at handling his emerging sexuality as a young person and has very little constructive input to give his own children. His own difficulties generate in him the fear that his children will have those same problems, which he wants to spare them.

This father has put the Act principles to work rather well when it comes to the sex education of his children, even though it is uncomfortable for him. He has *affirmed* that, despite the problems he had growing up, God wants his children to have a better sexual understanding than he had, and he has affirmed that he is responsible to provide that for them.

His *commitment* to action has taken many directions. He has done a considerable amount of study on his own to deal with some of his own ignorance. He has pursued counseling to work out some of the difficulties from his past. As part of his investigation he has discovered materials that are designed for use by children at various ages. He has provided these to his children. Furthermore, he has made it a point to explain to his children not only basic sexual information, but at least some of his own struggle as an adolescent. His weakness contributes to their strength.

He is in the position of *trusting* God for the results of his act of faith in being open with his teenage children about his own difficulties and providing adequate sexual information. And it is paying off. His older children have significant reputations among their peers for high moral standards—sometimes counseling friends in their questionable sex behavior. The risks he took were worth it in his children's lives.

Sexual Problems

Certain sexual problems with children are particularly troublesome. Girls need to be alerted to the dangers of rape; boys to the problem of being approached by homosexuals. Parental openness ahead of time can make all the difference in the world should these problems ever occur.

In no way should a child who has been sexually molested be made to feel guilt, shame, or doubt about himself. The experience itself will be traumatic enough without adding these problems. Do not hesitate to seek medical, legal, and psychological assistance if your child has had a sexually traumatic experience. No matter how you may feel, the real shame and blame is not on you or your child. The potential embarrassment is a small price to pay for the welfare of your child in this important area.

Pornography

Other sexual problems are more a question of personal and family responsibility. Pornography is easily accessible in our society.

Children need to know what this is and how dehumanizing it is. Should you find a nudie magazine under your son's mattress, this is a good opportunity to talk through the problem of pornography. A calm response on your part will promote his trust in you. Do not forget your struggles with this when you were his age and don't give an impression you went through all your teenage years with your glands out of gear. He knows better. Start by talking calmly. Seek to discover the attraction to your child in this material. Ask yourself if you, as a parent, need to give him more attention and affection. Talk about God's ideas for sex in marriage and identify how this material violates those ideals. Provide other reading materials that will give him the sex information he needs.

Remember that this can be an important step in growing up for your child. You'll want to handle it in a way that will answer the real questions and needs and will prevent a pattern of irresponsible attitudes from developing.

Though we would all like a world in which our children would not have to face these sorts of problems, that is not possible. The only way to protect children from the dangers of these sexual crises is with positive example and education. Our children must learn from us how to cope with evil in the world without being paralyzed by it. Running away will not work. Children cannot be kept ignorant and be expected to survive their confrontations with sin. We cannot put the lid on the barrel of explosives and sit on it. The explosion will be catastrophic. We must take each bomb out and defuse it.

One strict, conservative Christian family tried to shield their children from the negative influences of the world around them, particularly the school. One day their eight year old son came home from school and asked his mother what "rape" was. Rather than attempting some sort of explanation that he could understand, she told him that was a bad thing to ask about. They decided that the public school was too negative in its influence so they moved to another community where there was a Christian school.

The decision to send their child to a Christian school is not the problem here; that could have been an appropriate commitment to action. In this case it was unfortunately motivated by a desire to run from the problem, in hopes that it would go away. A better approach would have been to use this as an opportunity for further sex education and biblical understanding. Then, even in the public school, they could trust God to honor the moral foundation and teaching they had given their son as responsible Christian parents in a sinful world.

Teenage Pregnancy

Teenage promiscuity, especially when it leads to pregnancy, is one of the most serious sexual crises. Sadly, it is faced by hundreds of Christian families every year and requires parents to make one of the most demanding acts of faith of their lives.

Dealing with this problem must start by *affirming* your continued love for your son or daughter and that God has a way to deal with this. Even though the young couple has sinned, God has a positive plan for them. Though unpleasant decisions must be made, God is able to bring good from it.

Armed with the confidence of that affirmation of God's sovereignty, those involved can proceed to develop a plan of action. They can make some specific *commitments* to immediate steps. A quickie wedding is not usually the best solution to this problem. Statistics show a high divorce rate associated with being young and pregnant at the time of marriage.

A leading family of a fine evangelical church had been having trouble with a rebellious teenage daughter. She became pregnant, but marriage was unwise. These parents risked their reputations and the possible influence on their four younger children with a courageous act of faith. They were more concerned with their daughter's welfare than maintaining their own image which was a difficult decision.

They encouraged their daughter to keep her baby and invited her to live with them and offered to help her raise this new daughter. They extended the love of Christ at a tough time and at great personal sacrifice. That daughter matured and renewed her faith in Christ. Later she married a man who was both a responsible husband and father.

That was many years ago. The daughter and her husband have been one of the leading couples in one of the most prominent churches in their denomination for many years now. The granddaughter is now married and providing a Christian home for her own children. Her husband is an ordained minister in professional Christian service.

While a premarital pregnancy is never easy to handle, the experience of this family shows that God can be *trusted* to provide not just a way out of the problem but a positive outcome for His children. This in no way minimizes the reality and seriousness of the sin involved. It only affirms that even when caught in their sins, God has a constructive plan for His children. It requires a wise commitment to what may be very difficult choices.

The Parents Themselves

One positive step parents can take is getting together with other parents of teenagers to discuss what they are facing with their children. Together they can plan specific steps geared to the maturing of their own young people, especially if they are growing up in the same church.

Parents can commit themselves consciously to a stance and relationship with their teenager of being a supportive, guiding influence and overtly rejecting things that cast them in an adversary role. As Howard Hendricks frequently advises parents, "Get off your kid's back and get on his team."

A Parent's Faith

A parent's faith in Christ can be a significant resource in facing crises with his children. A question frequently asked is how a parent's faith affects the maturing faith of his children and their relationship with him.

Phillip Yancey of *Campus Life* Magazine offers some answers in a *Moody Monthly* article analyzing Merton Strommen's *Five Cries of Youth*. A group of Christian parents and their teenage children were given the same questionnaire on values. The parents were supposed to guess how their children would answer. Both were asked to describe their parent-child relationship. The answers of the teens and their parents were then compared.

How well were parents able to predict their teens' answers? What factors made parents better predictors? How did descriptions of the parent-child relationship compare? What is the relationship of the faith of the parent and the faith of the teen? Yancey interprets the results for Christian parents.

"As you might expect, the parents who had predicted a high percentage of their teenager's responses had the best relationship with their teenager. An understanding parent who accurately perceives his child can better meet his needs and relate more cordially.

"Some responses were shocking. One teenager, the child of a poorly correlating parent wrote: 'My mother is a witch, a snob, and a noisy Holy Roller. I despise her.' The mother showed incredible lack of perception by saying, 'My relationship with my teenager is a good one—we are close, and I feel she often confides in me and desires to please. We are pals.' (Undoubtedly, if the daughter exploded in anger and left home, the mother would be confused and hurt. She had completely misread her teenager.)"

Strommen concluded that the high-correlating parents with good relationships with their teens and the low-correlating parents with poor relationships with their teens "were very much alike in most areas under comparison. . . . Where they differed markedly was in their perception of the Christian faith. Low-correlating parents tended to view Christianity as a religion of works—something one did. The high-correlating parents tended to view Christianity as a religion of grace—something one accepts as a gift."

Strommen "has come up with a devastating question for evangelical parents. . . . 'Could it be that teenagers are rejecting their parents' faith because it is a faith based on works and not on grace?' One of the statements tested was, 'The main emphasis of the Gospel is on God's rules for right living.' More than half agreed! It's as if the Apostle Paul and Martin Luther had never opened their mouths!" (Phillip Yancey, "How Your Faith Affects Your Teenager," *Moody Monthly*, December, 1975.)

How can you tell if you are understanding your teenager accurately? One of the most telling, though sometimes painful, clues is whether your teen feels the freedom to disagree with you or to tell you negative things about your relationship. If this freedom exists without provoking anger, the relationship is probably healthy, and your teen will likely assimilate most of your values. If, in one way or another, you tell your child that you will not tolerate this sort of disagreement or negative input, you will drive it underground and stimulate rebellion. On the other hand, the freedom to accept this kind of input defuses it and brings you and your child together in a warm and wholesome relationship.

So this can be another conscious *commitment* that you make for your children in their teen years. Accept negative input from them, *trusting* God that this acceptance will result in an improving relationship. This particular commitment is based on the *affirmation* that the young person is a person in his own right with his own mind and his own right to his own opinons. It affirms that your home is a safe place and that you are the best people in the world for your young people to share both their positive and negative thoughts with.

A Marriage Crisis

Children bring another kind of crisis that is just too important not to mention. They can seriously affect your marriage. This can be acute if husband and wife are at odds on how to raise the children. Arland Thornton's study reports "empirical evidence suggesting that marital satisfaction decreases with the coming of children into the family.

"Children may create conflict, intensifying existing conflict, or decrease enjoyable marital interaction. Indeed, these considerations suggest that the indirect causal impact of children upon marital satisfaction may be negative rather than positive" ("Children and Marital Stability," *Journal of Marriage and the Family*, August, 1977, pp. 531ff).

As a parent, you can probably identify the conflicts and stresses children place on your marriage. They reduce opportunities for private communication, limit the time available for fellowship as a couple, and restrain sexual freedom. And these difficulties increase with the number of children. Wise parents plan in advance to give priority attention to their marriage over their children. Jesus said that a man leaves his father and mother and cleaves to his wife and nothing separates them (Mark 10:7-9), not even the children. Marriage is the permanent relationship—parenthood the temporary.

Affirm the value of each child, that each one is a special gift and creation of God. Affirm the value of your marriage, that God intends you to grow together even after children are born. *Commit* yourselves to actions that support your marriage. Plan special weekends away as a couple for refreshing and renewing your relationship. Have frequent dates to keep current on communication and to enjoy each other's company. Plan your routine for some privacy for the two of you each day. Then, *trust* God to meet the needs of your marriage and your children.

6

Climbing the Ladder

Pursuit of career success is fraught with crisis for the individual and the family. To win may be to lose, while not to try to win is unthinkable. One man whose story is told in *Passages,* offered this commentary: "I'm near the top of the mountain that I saw as a young man, and it's not snow. It's mostly salt. . . . Most guys I talk with who are successful . . . left their personal lives behind them. . . . Professionally, they're terrific, but their personal lives are in a mess" (Sheehy, *Passages,* p. 173).

Another man pinpointed the higher priority that is set aside in favor of career success when he remarked, "The next important thing to a man after his job, and even higher than his job if he will admit it . . . is the personal relationship with his woman. Why is that the area he's dying in?" (Sheehy, *Passages,* p. 174)

Gail Sheehy's commentary on these broken lives identifies the culprit. "A man must be faithful and endlessly attentive to his real loved one the career" (Sheehy, *Passages,* p. 155). In some ways, Christians can suffer from this problem even more than their totally secular neighbors. If they have taken seriously the teaching of the church, they are called by God to their vocation. To shirk here would be to disobey God. The church then goes on to add further guilt by demanding active participation in a ministry beyond the job.

Those with professional ministries often suffer most from this insatiable drive for success. Many families are almost destroyed by the father's ministry career. They are able to reverse the pattern only with determined action.

Ministry versus Family

One husband gave himself to his ministry with all the vigor that a rising young executive would give to climbing the corporate ladder, if not more. He perceived it as doing "God's work." Evenings and weekends were held as semisacred and devoted to work rather than family play.

The rapid arrival of several children placed enormous strain on his young wife. She was left to care for the home and children on her own, while the husband established his career and leadership in the church. Despite sincere efforts at loving discipline, the children became increasing behavior problems. When their teenage daughter ran away, they were motivated to reexamine their priorities and face their situation realistically.

This couple acted to deal with their crisis. They have consistently *affirmed* that it was God's plan for them to endure the struggles, many of which they made for themselves. They affirmed that God had a way for them to cope with the difficulties rather than giving up. Fortified by a sense of moral obligation to the permanency of their marriage, they persisted in their *commitment* to each other even when they had difficulty affirming that they were experiencing God's best for them.

Over the years they have made various commitments to action, including seeking professional counseling, but the primary commitment was to their marriage covenant. They have struggled together through the hard times with an eye toward better days ahead. They are *trusting* God for the outcome, and to honor their commitments.

Some of the scars remain. Their oldest child (now grown) still struggles with a sense of rejection and they are paying for the faulty priorities of their earlier life.

Their own marriage not only survived, but bloomed as they learned to control their involvements beyond the family and recognized impending stress before it reached crisis proportions.

Satisfying Job

While overcommitment to job and career is a source of crisis for the family, so is the inability to make at least tentative career choices. The search for a satisfying job can be one of the early marriage crises. Those who are well educated but lacking experience may be especially troubled by having to work at something less than their dreams and ambitions. A commitment to a plan of positive action can help a person gain experience, while looking for the right job.

It is interesting to note that the idea of one lifework is becoming increasingly obsolete. Alvin Toffler, author of *Future Shock,* suggests that people will not only be changing jobs more often, but increasingly they will be changing careers. Christians sometimes have a harder time dealing with this because of the understanding of God's calling to a vocation.

When the need for such a change becomes obvious, it can be quite traumatic. You may have serious doubts about your ability to discern God's leading, and may feel you wasted the time invested in your previous career or job.

Career Change

All organizations and companies go through stages and cycles of development. It is impossible and unhealthy to remain static. Times of transition place severe career stress on those involved. One Christian organization's restructuring altered the careers of several employees. For some, it was a time of growth and positive development, but for others, it launched a period of increasing difficulty. The circumstances would be somewhat different in a secular business, but the ways of coping with these changes would be similar.

The assistant to the chief executive was unsure of the action he should take when his boss stepped down. Since graduating from college, his entire career had been with the organization. To face the prospect of leaving was deeply traumatic for him in light of his abiding loyalty. Nevertheless, he suspected that submitting his resignation would be wise and healthy for the organization as well as for himself. He sought guidance of friends and went through a period of several weeks of difficult indecision.

When he resigned, he had no new career in mind. He wasn't even sure what he might be prepared and qualified to do. In the midst of this crisis he *affirmed* that God did have a place of effective ministry for him. His *commitment* to action was to begin sending job résumés to organizations and contacting friends throughout the United States. Feeling that he should move, he put his house up for sale and *trusted* God for response to his inquiries. Before long he had an offer from a Christian college where he has continued happily now for many years.

Another man left a little while later, feeling that the Holy Spirit was clearly leading him to make a change. He resigned without any clear sense of future direction, but convinced that God would not show him the next step until he took this first one.

The weeks stretched into months without anything solid developing. Anyone of lesser spiritual stature would surely have collapsed under this kind of pressure. But finally, after considerable contacts, a conference center engaged him as full-time director where he has been now for a number of years. He was strong on affirming that God had a plan and strong on trusting God to bring that plan to fruition. God has honored his faith and rewarded his current ministry.

Unfortunately, not all who changed careers in this transition fared so well. Another of the organization's top executives found a new career, but a troubled life.

Because of negative feelings over the way his release was handled, he sought new employment in the secular field. His reaction dulled his spiritual edge and his emphasis shifted more to professional qualifications than divine calling. He has built a successful career but at the expense of his spiritual vigor and family relationships. His marriage is now in crisis. He and his wife are separated. Denial has been his chief means of coping with these difficulties.

Another man was at the center of the upheaval. Though not entirely happy with the direction the organization was taking, he determined to work for what he believed, in a quiet but forceful manner.

Finally, he was relieved of his regular responsibilities and offered the opportunity to create a new job. During that time he pursued further education and explored the direction of his own life. He did not resign until he had another job in a secular college. The experience has been strengthening to his spiritual life and an opportunity for a new evangelistic ministry.

The whole pattern took about three years to develop. He *affirmed* that God had a plan into which he could constructively fit. He *committed* himself to staying until God provided the next step. He *trusted* that God would use and honor his faithfulness and loyalty. He trusted God to provide experiences that would be further enriching to his long-term career. This sort of commitment and trust were necessary to sustain him through what turned out to be a prolonged period of crisis.

Reactions

These four men responded in four different ways to the same circumstances that resulted in career changes for each of them. For three of them, the change was an act of faith that God rewarded. For all of them, the change had direct effects on their marriages and families. One husband-wife team worked together to provide family income during the transition. Another couple came apart.

The difference was not what kind of career change but how it was made. You will probably make two or three career changes during your lifetime. Depending on how you act when these times come, they can be the force of destruction or the life-force for your family. You can begin to work on your attitudes now so these changes will be positive opportunities, not signifying failure, but a realistic way to prolong vitality.

Unemployment

Unemployment is probably the greatest vocational crisis and can affect the whole family profoundly. During a period of widespread unemployment, social differences are minimized and everyone suffers, the poor most acutely.

A study was done of unemployed men and their families during the Great Depression of the 1930s. Its findings suggest a couple of ways to act that can help you prepare for or deal with unemployment.

The study's most important finding was that the basis of the man's authority in the family was strongly related to how well he and the whole family dealt with unemployment. It distinguished between "primary" authority and "instrumental" authority. Primary authority was defined as authority based on love and respect, while instrumental or utilitarian authority was seen as based on the man's role as provider (Mirra Komarovsky, *The Unemployed Man and His Family*. New York: Octagon Books, 1971, pp. 54-55).

These two terms are at the heart of acting in the face of unemployment. Apparently, the fate of the unemployed husband's authority depended largely on two factors—the predepression attitude of the wife and his own behavior during unemployment. Knowing this, a couple can work together as a team during times of unemployment for the benefit of their marriage and family. The wife contributes love and confidence to her husband. The husband makes constructive use of his time.

A Wife's Love

If you are a wife, your love for your husband is critical to preventing any future unemployment from damaging your marriage and family. Every wife should act to show love to her husband. She should value him as a person, not just an economic asset, and ask herself, "If my husband could not provide for the family materially, would my love for him be any less?" A wife's love protects her husband from the possible ravages of unemployment and also fulfills a command of the New Testament, given in Titus 2:4.

Two wives' comments about their husbands were quoted in the study. As you read their words watch for their attitudes of love and for actions taken by their husbands.

"Mrs. Lake said, 'Since unemployment, my husband does more for us than ever. He tries hard to make the children love him, and make me feel more towards him. He simply cannot do enough for us. I know that he tries, and I don't know why he should for he knows that we all love him.' The wife feels that he is an ideal husband, even if he is out of work. He always does what she asks him to do—plays with the children when they are cranky, and tries to amuse them. The man is very much perturbed about the needs of the family, but attempts to control his worry and irritability, and has become more tender to the family.

"Mrs. Brown noted that since unemployment she has become nervous and has had spells of irritation, but her husband has been more patient with her than ever. He has done his 'darndest' to get the family out of the depression. Whenever she has had the blues, he encouraged her and told her how loyal she had been and how much he appreciated her cooperation. He told her that she was an understanding woman and much better than most wives. He has been more attentive to her than he used to be" (Komarovsky, *The Unemployed Man and His Family,* p. 677).

If a husband has the supportive love of his wife when he is out of work, he is then free to devote himself to loving his family too. This liberates him to deal with the other crisis of unemployment—idle time. He can act to use his time constructively: looking for work, doing odd jobs, building family relationships.

How can you and your spouse act in the face of unemployment? *Affirm* that each of you has value as persons, not just as income earners. Affirm that your marriage and family relationships are more important than work and material provision. *Commit* yourselves to express love and affection to each other and your children, no matter how hard your circumstances are. Commit yourselves to make good use of your time. *Trust* God to provide for you. After all, the Source of your life is not your work, effort, or intelligence, but God.

Financial Pressure

Unemployment usually creates financial pressure on the family. Other things beyond our control, such as unexpected illness or accidents, can increase the strain as well. The right action can minimize the damage and turn the crisis into an opportunity. If financial difficulties are caused by irresponsibility, action is needed to break out of the destructive pattern and establish new fiscal habits.

Believe it or not, the amount of money available is not usually the central issue at a time of financial crisis, except in cases of genuine poverty. The real problem is how that money is used. Most of us are not trained as money managers. Seeking assistance from a knowledgeable person in your congregation or from your bank is often a wise move.

One man was a creative and aggressive salesman. Early in his career he was involved in a number of business ventures involving personal financial risk beyond his ability and assets. As one after another of these projects failed, he found himself personally liable for sizeable debts. As a result he was considered a poor credit risk and was unable to purchase a home for his family for a number of years.

He was an excellent salesman and had no difficulty making good money, though he was a poor manager. He and his wife established sloppy habits of personal financial management, which were inadequate for dealing with the sizeable debt.

Eventually, they were able to purchase a home on a rent-with-option-to-buy-arrangement. Then came unexpected medical problems, and the bills increased. They began to have serious problems with bad checks and late payments.

In response to the stress of this situation, he left his high paying job to start a number of new small private ventures. As before, they all failed. He was once again faced with staggering debt. After missing several payments on the house, foreclosure proceedings were started. Help that was offered by some close friends who knew of the situation was rejected and the friendships cooled.

In many ways, this family's approach to their financial problems was the opposite of the Act principle. A sense of panic was substituted for the *affirmation* of God's way out of the problem. And at the same time the dependence on God was replaced by self-sufficiency. They rejected help from friends, sought to resolve the difficulty by dishonesty and with bad checks. There was a lot of activity but little *commitment* to a plan of action. The pattern was one of attempting to deal with each individual situation on its own in an escapist manner without regard to their total situation and without a comprehensive plan. This showed a lack of *trust* that God could honor a responsible approach to their debts. Each decision seemed to be an increasing statement of, "we will take care of ourselves," rather than depending on God. As the situation deteriorated, their actions became increasingly irresponsible and compounded their problems.

Moving

Moving is another event that can precipitate considerable family crisis. For whatever reason you move, it will have a major impact on your family. It is tiring for everyone, leaving nerves raw and tempers short. The parade of realtors, lawyers, prospective buyers, movers, and friends leaves you exhausted and jittery. You have old relationships to close off and new ones to make. Finding a new church is often involved.

Your children will change schools and making that transition can be crucial for their continued academic and social development.

Early one summer, one of our staff men with a son just starting junior high school was planning a move. The school principal suggested the transition be made as easy as possible. "The last choice," he said, "is to move in the middle of the year. The second choice is to move in the spring after he has finished his first year here. But the best time to move would be this summer, before school starts. That way he could stay in the same school for his whole junior high school experience."

Moving is becoming common. We are experiencing a migration similar to when the western frontier was opening up a little less than a century ago. About 20 percent of the U.S. population moves each year. Of course, people in certain professions are on the move much more frequently than others. Military families are lengendary for frequent, inopportune moves. But all this moving is not necessarily damaging. It can be an opportunity for an expanded education and building a wealth of friendships.

One father, who works for an airline, moves his family almost every year. The children go to a new school every year: all new friends, a completely new situation. Immediately, the children become involved in the school activities, the church, Sunday School, the young people's group. These kids get elected to the offices in their church and at school. Some have become class presidents in the year they attend a particular school. Every community, every church, every school misses them when they leave. Obviously, this family has made up its mind that God has the solution to this problem. They have committed themselves to taking the initiative in building new relationships when they are in a new place. The crisis becomes an opportunity.

7

Male and Female Partnership

The women's movement has received media attention in recent years and the struggles within many marriages have swollen to a public contest between men and women. This chapter is not going to define a position on a woman's special function, nor is it going to delineate a theology of headship and submission. Plenty of other books already do those things. Instead, I want to tell you how you can act to turn the crisis of competition over roles in your marriage into cooperation and partnership.

The rhetoric over the place of women in the home, church, and world seldom addresses the few practical and specific areas where differences over roles affect your marriage. What is the effect of a working wife on your family? How do you divide up responsibilities in the home? How do you make decisions in your family? Do your answers to these questions generate harmony or strife in your marriage?

I am much more concerned with how your action affects your marriage than I am with purely following an abstract principle. For instance, my wife and I have had a pretty traditional role relationship. She has always had a strong conviction against her working outside the home, even though she has had a speaking ministry for many years. But we decided to make an exception once a number of years ago. Only one of the boys was still home. She was having some real health problems, but I felt she was getting too wrapped up in herself and her ailments. I took a risk and said, "I think you need to get a job." This was contrary to everything she believed and we had a real struggle with it. I didn't tell her why I made the suggestion because she would have assumed that I wasn't taking her illnesses seriously.

Knowing her genuine love for people, I knew that if she ever got into the marketplace she'd become involved in helping others and forget some of her own difficulties. So I insisted, "You've got to do it right away." She refused adamantly but finally said, "I think you are mistaken but I will do it because I believe you are the family leader—but you must take total responsibility for whatever happens as a result."

She got a job at an exclusive gift shop, which was exactly what she needed. She's vivacious and outgoing and could sell mittens to a fish. The job changed her whole schedule and daily structure as well as many other things.

She began to change noticeably. She wasn't working more than three days before she came home and said, "You know, Elsie at the shop really needs help. I'm burdened for that woman." Soon she became involved and concerned with other people and began to witness and pray for them. Her conversations began to center around them and their needs instead of her own. She came out of her shell, and her employment served a very significant purpose in our marriage. We made the necessary adjustments during a critical period and actual roles were not as important as the overall relationship.

Marriage Oneness

Marriage is a partnership of two complementary individuals, and each has given him or herself to love and serve the other. Since Old Testament times the biblical writers have used the husband-wife relationship to illustrate God's relationship to His people (Hosea; Jer. 31:21, 32; 2 Cor. 11:2; Eph. 5:21-33; Rev. 21:9).

In marriage, the couple becomes a new entity, a total partnership. The Bible's marriage manifesto is stated in Genesis 2:24: "Therefore shall a man leave his father and his mother and shall cleave unto his wife; and they shall be one flesh" (KJV). Oneness is a characteristic and priority of marriage. This passage is quoted in the New Testament four times (Matt. 19:5; Mark 10:7-8; 1 Cor. 6:16; Eph. 5:31), and it is clear that whatever disrupts this relationship of oneness is contrary to God's intent.

The question of role and authority in marriage is secondary to oneness. If conflict over roles threatens the unity of marriage, it is wrong, no matter how right one's position on roles may be. With this in mind, flexibility to act is the key to unity.

Rigid ideas of what is distinctly masculine or feminine are destructive. They prevent the give-and-take required to work out a harmonious partnership. They are degrading to both men and women. Any time a person's worth is assigned a given role, he is demeaned when he is unable to fulfill that role.

Working Wives and Finances

Our society attaches inordinate importance to economic success. All too often it is used as a gauge of personal worth. Money is often the driving force behind one of the most common and troublesome role conflicts in marriage: the working wife.

The image of the woman who never takes a job outside the home but devotes her entire life to caring for her husband and children is becoming a romantic fiction. "Thirty-five is when the average married American woman reenters the working world. Census figures show she can then expect to be part of the work force for the next twenty-four years or more" (Gail Sheehy, *Passages,* p. 379).

Lois Wladis Hoffman reports that "Women give 'money' as their major reason for working" ("The Decision to Become a Working Wife," *Family Roles and Interaction,* Jerold Heiss, ed. Chicago: Rand McNally, 1968, p. 237). Robert O. Blood, Jr. confirms this finding with his observation. "Economic necessity is the chief reason for working given by working wives. However, 'necessity' is a slippery term in an advertising-saturated culture. Nevertheless, in general, the lower the husband's income, the greater the necessity for the wife to supplement it. And the greater the necessity for her paid activity, the less resentment for the loss of her unpaid services at home" (Blood, "The Effect of the Wife's Employment on the Husband Wife Relationship," *Family Roles and Interaction,* p. 258).

The actual amount of money available to the family does not make as much difference as the standard of living the family attempts to maintain, which is usually set by those around them. Hoffman notes that "Women are motivated to work when they define their husband's incomes as inadequate . . . and will go to work to maintain their standard of living, or will also take employment to achieve the level of those around them" (Hoffman, p. 236-237).

A man stood up in one of our large seminars and asked a question about money. He remarked that with the economy and inflation the way they are, both husband and wife have to work, not because they want to but because of necessity. Their schedules are full and time together is limited. He asked, "How can we make family principles work and build a real family time?" And said, "Our financial situation affects these other things."

A woman agreed, "What he's talking about is very real. A lot of us here at the seminar are really struggling with that. How practical is the whole idea of 'Seek ye first the kingdom of God and all these other things will be added'?"

Finances become the identified source of a lot of other problems. We're getting more and more to the place where we expect to live at a certain level of affluence, and in order to do that we think we need those two incomes. How much of that is in the economy, or how much is in the fact that we've had this era of prosperity and believe we should always be able to live at this luxury level?

The choice of life-style is the issue. Some people who are living at an income level of $15,000 to $20,000 per year are saying, "If we had another $5,000 or $10,000 we could really do something," while other people are earning $10,000 to $13,000 or less, and live economically all the time, no matter what. It's a matter of recognizing that Parkinson's law applies to money too: "Work expands so as to fill the time available for its completion." You won't have any more money to spend no matter how much you make.

As discussed in the last chapter, economic pressures can propel your family into a variety of crises. If raising your standard of living is your only motivation for working as a wife, perhaps you need to choose a more frugal life-style. Though money is the most common reason given for a wife to work, that can produce a number of other kinds of crises in the marriage.

For instance, "Is the financial motivation related to a feeling that the father is a failure? If so, the mother's employment could symbolize his failure for the whole family. On the other hand, the mother's employment could be part of cooperative planning and perceived as a symbol of family unity. Perhaps the working mother is paying penance for her poor management and extravagance. Or, she might want an independent income because of marital difficulties or simply out of a desire for autonomy in an otherwise close and congenial relationship" (Hoffman, p. 238).

Blood reports that "Dual-income couples quarrel more frequently than one-income couples. When conflict occurs in working-wife families, it does not spread randomly over all aspects of marriage. For instance, there is no increase in difficulties over in-laws, friendships, or sexual or religious matters. Almost all the significant differences are concentrated in the 'domestic-economic' field. Dual-income couples quarrel over money not because of the extra income but in spite of it" (Blood, pp. 263-264).

If any of these problems are plaguing you, can you Act to resolve them? Will you *affirm* that your marriage is more important than the standard of living you are pursuing? Will you affirm that God has a way for you to have a rich and satisfying marriage relationship, even if you are both working?

What kinds of *commitments* will you make to bring those affirmations to reality? Perhaps some of the income from the second job could be invested in regular evenings and weekends together. Perhaps you need to plan carefully for using your holidays and vacations for the maximum benefit of the whole family, including children. Possibly you could use one of the many programs available in churches and communities for marriage communication training.

These plans of action will not work out the same for every family. The secret is to work on them together.

It Can Be Done

Two couples with wives more educated than their husbands have taken different approaches, largely due to the differences in their stage of life.

One couple has been most successful in their role adjustments. She earned a doctorate and has a major decision-making role in a prominent Christian organization. Her lengthy career has consisted of several prestige jobs. The husband has no higher education and has always moved and adjusted to his wife's career. He has been a

laborer in a variety of fields and is now the supervisor of a main-
tenance crew for a large building. They are in their late fifties
and active in their very traditional church, where younger couples
hold them in high regard.

A younger couple has made a traditional role adjustment with
which they are satisfied, even though it is the source of chronic
financial difficulties. The husband is diligent, though uneducated,
and has had a series of unskilled jobs. His wife has a master's
degree and has turned down job opportunities to be at home with
the children. Though their income is severely limited, she has
acted to supplement it with long-term baby-sitting and custom bak-
ing. If she became the provider, they would double their income.
Though they are responsible about their financial situation, they
are plagued with chronic minor money problems and live in less
than ideal conditions. The children are getting older and soon all
will be in school. The wife is beginning to explore the possibilities
of getting a job to use her education. He is a good, loving father in
terms of both recreation and discipline with his children.

Valuing highly the intensive attention the mother can give the
children during their preschool years, they have chosen to live
on a much lower level than their neighbors. They have taken action
to give their relationship to their children higher priority than
providing them with things or a "nice" house. The wife has taken
action to help out financially with careful management and in-
home work. She is now looking forward to getting work when
all the children are in school, and is preparing for this with some
evening courses.

When They Are All in School

When the children are in school, many mothers find their sense of
satisfaction in the mothering role declines. "The period when the
youngest child enters school can be very difficult for many
mothers." They are "left with a day full of housework rather than
mothering" (Hoffman, p. 243). An outside job for such women
can be very important to their sense of making a meaningful contribution to their families.

James Olthuis, a teacher at the Institute for Christian Studies in
Toronto, expresses what many two-career families have known for
a long time. "Many families are discovering that the mother's

pursuit of outside interests makes her more attentive, understanding, and relaxed at home. Enjoying such experiences and growing through them, the mother develops herself more fully as a person. She is able to keep pace with her husband and growing family" (James Olthuis, *I Pledge You My Troth*, New York: Harper and Row, 1975, p. 104).

One such family had three children born in five years, so the last child was born just as the oldest child started school. Though this wife was highly educated, the time demands of the three young children kept her at home for the first eleven years of their marriage. She really enjoyed a number of the things that she was doing and having time with the children, but the total load was too much. She found herself getting increasingly short with the children and annoyed with anything that disrupted her daily routine of work.

By the time the youngest child started school and the older ones were ready to have more substantial chores, she went back to work as a public school teacher. Though this might seem to make the overload worse and shortchange the children, in their situation she became a much better mother when she went back to work. She was able to interact with adults so that the conversation with her children was not as trying. With the help of the older ones at first, and finally all three children, she was able to organize the week so that all the work could be done with more time available for all of them than they had before. As a teacher who did not work summers, she was free to spend the entire summer every year with her children, which were great times for the family.

As a young mother, she faced the crisis of coping with herself and her family by *affirming* that God had something meaningful for her in her career and as a mother. Looking forward to this in the future, she was sustained through a very trying period with her young children. She *committed* herself to action both by taking the job once all the children were in school, and by planning to make her time as valuable as possible for the entire family. She felt an obligation in terms of stewardship and general responsibilities to make a significant investment of her own time, ability, and education, as well as to build more positive relationships with her children. She took a specific action to accomplish these objectives, and *trusted* God to provide the strength, wisdom, and insight necessary to manage a job and her responsibilities at home. After a time at work she even had the opportunity to return to school and pursue a master's degree.

When a wife goes back to work after the children are all in school, both husband and wife must act together to keep this from precipitating a crisis in the family. The first action is to decide together that the wife is to seek a job. The husband must be supportive of his working wife if the transition is to go smoothly. His attitude and action must be clearly positive and his help with the household and childcare tasks will be needed to ease her burden at home.

The plan of action should even include the children. Older children can assume greater responsibility. They are often happy to do so, as they appreciate taking a more adult role in the family. In this way, when mother works, all share in both the work and the fun. Times together can be planned for maximum value. If the children discover they enjoy their relationship with their mother more when she is working, they will anticipate and value their times together.

None of this is intended to imply that all mothers should work, just as earlier suggestions were not intended to convey the thought that no mothers should ever work. Every family's situation is different. If having both husband and wife work seems necessary to you, don't let it become a crisis. Recognize the problems: tighter scheduling, arguments over money, differences of expectations, increased work for other family members. Consider the benefits you expect to gain. Measure them not only against the known costs, but also against your priorities and values. Whatever decisions you make, remember the priority of oneness from Genesis 2:24.

Complementary Roles

Role crises are not resolved in marriage by one partner doing what he thinks is right, without regarding the perspective of his spouse. Couples must work together from the start with patience and humility. Imposing your will on your partner or insisting on your own way is a sure way to compound a crisis. Basic selfishness is our biggest problem. Paul's great passage on marriage and the church begins with these words: "Be subject to one another in the fear of Christ" (Eph. 5:21), and this sets the tone for other instructions for couples in the following verses. By submitting to each other, you can work through any role crisis.

What then is the source of role conflict and crisis in marriage? The difficulty is not with a particular philosophy or perspective on roles. Rather, husbands and wives operate on different sets of assumptions and expectations. These may be either differing views of roles or conflicting patterns of behavior.

Studies indicate that "a substantial number of husbands and wives experience role attitude-behavior incongruence." While "both sexes tend to express role-sharing attitudes . . . women enact the majority of duties related to all roles with the exception of the provider role, which is mainly performed by men" (Sharon K. Araji, "Husbands and Wives' Attitude Behavior Congruence on Family Roles," *Journal of Marriage and the Family,* May 1977, pp. 309ff.) Both married men and women express role-sharing attitudes but this is not generally reflected in role behaviors, especially on the part of men.

This study points directly to the need for action. If you are experiencing conflict over roles in your marriage, you need to change your behavior. I suspect that most often the husband is the one with the greatest change to make. That's been true in my case. Verbal affirmations of your wife's gifts and abilities are fine, but need to be accompanied by real opportunities to use them. Verbal agreement that you should share in household duties is meaningless unless you are actually taking responsibility for specific tasks.

Even if you do not achieve complete agreement on a philosophy of roles, you can work together to agree on a plan of harmonious action. You can discuss who will take responsibility for specific jobs in the household with a spirit of cooperation and loving service. This must start with the affirmation that you are working toward unity in marriage where each is seeking the best for the other. You *affirm* that God has a way for you to work together as partners. The beginning of *commitment* is to open yourself to changes in the pattern of behavior that has been troublesome to you. Then work together on just one or two changes at a time to adjust your patterns. *Trust* God to give you insights into what commitments to make and to give you the attitude and fortitude to hold to them.

You do not need to feel confined to your background or locked into the pattern that is now a source of conflict for you. You *can* change, and the most important influence on your change will be your spouse. That is exactly as it should be. If you are committed to God's plan for marriage oneness (Gen. 2:24), you will want your spouse to change you. You can even plan and pace that change by working together.

One of the things that we each carry from our background is an identification of certain activities as being uniquely male or female. We learned these things early in life as we observed our parents. Changing these patterns is not easy, but it can be done for the benefit of your marriage. These differences in expectations can cause tension and awkwardness if they are not faced openly, with a good dose of humor.

Who Works the Garden?

In one suburban church, the pastor was attempting in a sermon to demonstrate the creative and positive things women could do in the family as they fulfilled their uniquely feminine household responsibilities. In this list he included caring for the garden. Because he has no interest at all in yardwork and his wife maintains a nice garden of both vegetables and flowers, he identified this as a feminine task. The church property, however, includes several large garden plots operated by families in the congregation. These plots are all managed by the men in those families, though several of the wives do work with their husbands. In this case, the expectations for the role involvement were different from family to family and resulted in a little bit of tension in the congregation. Individual families felt that their understanding was right and concluded that the other families who have different perspectives were somehow distorting biblical sex roles.

The lists of jobs that have been assigned to one sex in one family and the other sex in another family could go on indefinitely: taking out the garbage, scrubbing the floors, painting and decorating, changing the baby, washing dishes. Sociology professor John Peters tells of the transformation in his marriage when he began to take on some of the jobs his wife had previously done.

"Increasingly, I have become aware of the heavy responsibility and energy involved in running a household with five children. Should I be surprised that my wife often has been exhausted when involved in home and outside activities? To ease this situation, I am now responsible for preparing breakfast. But so ingrained was the 'motherly role,' that at first my wife felt guilty for 'allowing me' this change in pattern. Now we are both content with this arrangement. The children and I also have assumed other housekeeping jobs, but even today it is hard for my wife to relinquish some household duties. We finally are beginning to see that we are not 'doing mother's work,' but that keeping the house is a family affair" ("Male Chauvinist in Retreat," *Christian Life Magazine,* October 1977, pp. 26 ff).

Making Decisions

John Peters has caught the idea of oneness in marriage and the family. He took some real action to build up his wife. Their sense of unity extended to their pattern of decision-making. If any area of marriage should be characterized by a spirit of cooperation in marriage, it is making decisions that affect the whole family. Throughout the Bible harmony and unity in marriage are of higher priority than a sense of hierarchy. To allow an abstract philosophy of headship and submission, or an arbitrary list of who makes what decision to disrupt marital oneness, would be a grievous error.

It is frequently argued that someone must have the last word if a couple cannot come to an agreement, and that this better be known in advance of the crisis. Perhaps so, and I would say that the husband holds this "wild trump" in the case of any impasse or stalemate. But often, this can be an excuse for not working hard enough to come to agreement. It may show a lack of commitment to being a couple. This prerogative should only be used in extreme situations a very few times throughout a couple's whole married life. Notice what happened to John Peter's marriage when he began sharing the decision-making with his wife more fully.

"I used to make most of the family decisions. I do not think I was autocratic, because I usually consulted my wife. But we are most careful to feel each other out now, and in many cases my wife makes the decision, though at times she finds this difficult. She wonders if she is capable, whether she has weighed all the angles. Because she is unaccustomed to this responsibility, her leap is often frightening. Neither of us feels the need to always be right or to be the final decision-maker. I am freer to talk to my wife about male cultural restraints such as bearing the responsibility of economic support, the pressure to succeed professionally, to always be rational, and restrain emotion. As a result she is more understanding of me" (Peters, pp. 26ff.).

As you know by this time, I have avoided direct comment on the current women's movement. I do think we as Christians need to be very careful in our analysis. Wholesale condemnation or adoption of its agenda would be foolish and would cheat the church of the opportunity to learn and grow.

It is intriguing that a few generations back, Christians were the leaders of three related movements: temperance, abolition, and sufferage. The modern civil rights and women's movements grew out of these roots, though few evangelical Christians are attempting to speak God's Word in those settings any more. If nothing else, the women's movement should challenge Christian couples, and especially men, to a new vitality of marriage oneness.

Author and speaker Charlie Shedd makes an interesting observation. "Is there any man who understands all the current feminist movement? I doubt it. But I know one thing they're about, and I know because I asked them. The bunch I asked last Saturday are considerably fed up with the men they've known well. Like husbands, fathers. Strictly for dads, I think women's lib is men's fault. Had we been urging the gals to do their thing, we would long ago have given them the liberties to which they are entitled. We would have heralded their uniqueness. Many a dumb male has used the female for all he could get out of her. No wonder she rose up to say, 'Look, Buster, I'm something more than an appendage to you.'

"I'm not for unisex. No way! Let us praise the Lord that He made male and female. But any man with his head screwed on these days will say to his woman, 'There is plenty of room for us to love each other, have a family, and you still be you" (Charlie Shedd, *The Best Dad Is a Good Lover*. Mission, Kansas: Sheed Andrews and McMeel, 1977, pp. 89, 92).

8

Coming Apart at the Seams

Few tragedies are as excruciating as the death of a marriage and the ensuing divorce. Yet many more couples live in silent isolation without ever appearing as a divorce statistic. Even the most healthy couples encounter conflict occasionally. Evelyn and I do, and I'm sure you do too. How can you learn to manage your conflicts so they do not escalate and demolish your marriage? If your conflicts have become a runaway crisis, how can you call a halt and begin putting it back together? If you are in the throes of divorce, how can you live meaningfully from this point forward?

The answers to these questions do not come easily. Outside professional help often is needed to rebuild relationships when husbands and wives have been effectively destroying each other. Negative patterns of thought and action must be changed. In such a situation, it is difficult to see your own blind spots and hindering attitudes, and to know what to do to change them. The impact of marital estrangement reaches far beyond the two of you. Children need special tools to help them cope with conflict between their parents.

Crises can be opportunities for growth, if you will use them constructively, and marital conflicts are no different. Up to this point, I have discussed how various crises can have a positive or negative effect on your marriage and family. Now I want to consider your marriage relationship itself. In the same way, the marriage conflicts you have can either escalate to full-scale crises, perhaps even divorce, or they can serve to build a stronger partnership and a richer intimacy. The difference is how you choose to act.

Dr. John Scanzoni explains how conflict can be a tool for building a healthy marriage. "Conflict brings into the open the issue that one or the other partner considers unjust or inequitable. If it is brought into the open, bargained over, and resolved so that the result is satisfactory to both partners, their relationship reverts back to one based on ongoing reciprocities, and therefore solidarity and stability. . . . Marital conflicts, in other words, may enhance stability because they may lead to *change,* by removing the sources of conflict" (John Scanzoni, *Sexual Bargaining,* Englewood Cliffs: Prentice Hall, 1972, p. 75).

Conflict is certainly not pleasant, but it can be a stepping-stone to growth in your relationship if it is the transition from one stage of development to another. Conflict becomes constructive when it is resolved with some positive change. And change requires action.

Basic and Nonbasic Conflict

Scanzoni also distinguishes between basic and nonbasic conflict. Some conflicts are intrinsic threats to your marriage, demanding immediate and drastic attention. Others are troublesome and can be worked at in a more relaxed fashion. You will usually be able to deal with nonbasic conflicts yourselves, if there is a strong commitment to the relationship and a willingness to act.

What is basic conflict? "Most Americans . . . expect that if he is healthy, the husband is *obligated* to fulfill the provider role. Suppose, however, that a husband unilaterally decided to 'drop out of the rat race,' to quit his job and cease entirely to work or to function in his role as provider. The wife will very likely consider this behavior *unfair* and conflict is thereby ignited. Since it is not likely that the wife can physically coerce her husband to return to work, and if she herself does not wish to work, then the only lever of 'power' left to her is to threaten to leave him. If this does not alter his behavior, it is then very likely that their marriage could end in divorce" (Scanzoni, *Sexual Bargaining,* p. 73).

Basic conflict "strikes at the core of the marital structure." It challenges the "basic consensus, or the rules of the game." Without rapid resolution, the marriage will dissolve under such pressure. Usually, professional help or a third party is necessary to resolve this kind of basic problem.

On the other hand, nonbasic conflicts do not directly threaten the marriage foundation. They still need resolution, but they do not demand such urgent and intensive attention.

For example, "the wife may want her husband to change jobs, to get one that will supply a better living standard for the family, whereas he wants to stay in his present job. She may consider it unfair of him to do so, while he may deem it unjust for her to push him in this fashion. Conflict erupts and both partners utilize whatever power they possess to try to achieve their goals. But since the husband is working, the conflict is over something comparatively less central (though very important)—the *kind* of job to work at. We might therefore assume that conflict of this sort is less likely to lead to total dissociation than where he refuses to work" (Scanzoni, *Sexual Bargaining,* p. 74).

When marital conflict is unresolved, estrangement and isolation are the result, often followed by separation or divorce. The best way to avoid a crisis of these proportions is to stay current in your marital relationship—keeping short accounts. Ignoring or neglecting seemingly small conflicts can be serious in spite of all the positive aspects of your marriage.

A well-known couple, Christian leaders, had a great marriage except for one unresolved problem. Whenever it came up they pushed it aside and concentrated only on the positive things in their relationship. They wrote good books on marriage and family life, conducted seminars, and helped many couples in their marriages. But their own difficulty remained unattended. It finally became too big to handle and drove a deep wedge between them. They are now divorced.

Act Together

Apply the Act principle. *Affirm* God's purpose for the unity of your marriage. Affirm that God has a way for you to resolve your differences and that you will not ignore them or pretend they don't exist. Affirm your differences as God's gifts and opportunities for your growth.

Commit yourself to constructive action. Take the risk and talk to each other about the problem. Phrasing your comments as *your* problem rather than your partner's will help keep emotions under control. Attack the problem rather than your partner. Criticizing your partner only compounds the disagreement. No one person is totally responsible for the problem.

Try to identify the source of the problem, not the person to blame. Together, brainstorm a list of actions you could take to resolve the conflict, without evaluating whether any of them are workable. Write them out on a piece of paper. Then go back and sort through the possible solutions, eliminating those that are clearly not going to help. Formulate a plan from the ones that are left. This might be a combination of several ideas, or one good one. Finally, agree to try the plan for a specific, usually brief period of time. Remember that both of you should be satisfied with the plan and fully committed to try it. After the set time, evaluate your progress and make necessary adjustments.

This works fine if both of you are willing to work and change for the sake of your marriage. It requires that you value your marriage commitment and relationship more than whatever is separating you at the time.

If one of you is unwilling to cooperate in the problem-solving, you are faced with a *basic* conflict. Unfortunately, in these cases, the uncooperative partner is frequently unwilling to seek outside help and the one suggesting counseling may be more interested in a supporting ally than in resolving the crisis.

When one or both of you are thwarting the problem-solving, you must begin by taking responsibility for yourself. Resist the urge to critique and blame your partner. Instead, ask yourself, "Am I fully accepting my partner even though we disagree? Am I withholding love and affection until things go my way? What am I doing to prevent the resolution of this crisis? What can I do to reverse that trend?" Once you see yourself more clearly, you can act in faith and trust God to work.

The Right Spirit

Remember the woman mentioned in chapter 2 who did not go along with her husband's divorce request? She determined "to be pleasant. After all, I had insisted the marriage continue. In all fairness, I had no right to make it unpleasant, no matter how wronged I felt." This is reflective of the spirit of the Apostle

Peter's words, "In the same way, you wives, be submissive to your own husbands so that even if any of them are disobedient to the word, they may be won without a word by the behavior of their wives, as they observe your chaste and respectful behavior. And let not your adornment be external only—braiding the hair, and wearing gold jewelry, and putting on dresses; but let it be the hidden person of the heart, with the imperishable quality of a gentle and quiet spirit, which is precious in the sight of God" (1 Peter 3:1-4). This same respectful behavior and gentle and quiet spirit would also be necessary for husbands in conflict with uncooperative wives.

This is the only approach that offers genuine hope if you are the only one interested in resolving the crisis of your marriage. It is the foundation on which you can build a trust in God for still unseen results. A program of personal counseling also can help you grow and cope with your emotions at such a time, but do not use the counselor as someone to "take your side."

Is Divorce a Solution?

For some of you, the crisis may have progressed to the point where divorce is being consciously considered or openly pursued. Restating the New Testament stance on divorce will probably not be convincing, though this is always the standard. You can read it for yourself in Matthew 5:31-32; 19:3-11; Mark 10:2-12; Luke 16:18; 1 Corinthians 7:10-17.

Divorce is often seen as the solution to the problems of an unsatisfactory marriage. People feel that "all the bad things will go away if I get divorced." That is never true. Divorce brings with it a host of new problems: financial pressure, hassles over children's visitation, legal implications, finding a new identity, changes in friendship patterns, working through deep grief. You cannot get rid of the unresolved problems of self by getting rid of the person on whom you have been projecting them.

Divorce should not be used as an escape mechanism, because you cannot run away from yourself. You must face up to your shortcomings and analyze your own failures before tackling those of your partner. This is perhaps the most important lesson you can learn if you are going through or recovering from a divorce. One author comments, "The superficial reason for their split seldom holds up once he has learned more about himself. It has very little to do with his wife, whoever she was" (Gail Sheehy, *Passages,* p. 209). Your own selfish contribution to the divorce must be confessed to God too.

At the point of divorce, the last vestige of unity in your marriage is dissolved. To continue affirming this is an illusion; you must shift your emphasis to *affirming* that God still has a plan for you, no matter how you have failed. You can affirm that He has something for you to learn and change about yourself. While divorce is hardly God's ideal way to gain realistic self-appraisal, to miss it would be to waste your pain.

The *commitment* you must make is first to allow yourself to grieve for your dead marriage. Then commit yourself to honest self-appraisal and the desire to overcome the things for which you were responsible in your divorce. Don't try to do it alone: a counselor or pastor is necessary and the supportive fellowship of your church is critical.

These steps may be the exact opposite of what you feel like doing. You will want to hide, isolate yourself, and nurse your wounds. Keep in mind that your friends and relatives are suffering with your loss too. They are confused as to how to respond to you. *Trust* God to use them to rebuild the warmth of relationships, to remove the fear of intimacy, and to lead you to something positive and beautiful for your broken life.

Jesus saves, comforts, and heals when He confronts broken, hurting people. Interestingly, He saves the harsh words for the self-righteous, the hypocrites. To the woman caught in adultery, Jesus said, "Neither do I condemn you; go your way; from now on sin no more" (John 8:11). To the hemorrhaging woman He said, "Your faith has made you well; go in peace, and be healed" (Mark 5:34). Of the prostitute who washed His feet with her tears, Jesus said, "Her sins, which are many, have been forgiven, for she loved much; but he who is forgiven little, loves little." And He said to her, "Your sins have been forgiven. . . . Your faith has saved you; go in peace" (Luke 7:47-50).

Sexual Conflict

A wry cliché states, "When a marriage is on the rocks, the rocks are usually in the bed." As you've discovered by this time, many things besides sex can disrupt a marriage. Sex is not the most important element in marriage, but without it, marriage would not be the unique relationship that it is. And sex can be either the culmination (a true climax) of your intimacy or the most intensive battleground for your marriage struggle.

Sexual crises in marriage are usually the result of conflicts over questions like frequency, technique, and initiation, or as dysfunctions such as impotence for men and being nonorgasmic for women. Both problems are so intermingled that they feed on each other. Every couple has difficulty with some of these things during their marriage. This should not be cause for alarm but a signal for some constructive action.

The most important sex organ is the brain. Our attitudes affect our sexual relationship more than anything else. Attitudes must be built on reliable information, so commit yourselves to getting more information. Good books from Christian authors are readily available.

I find two destructive attitudes common among Christian couples. First, the wife is not expected to desire or enjoy sex too much. She then represses her sexual urges and forces her husband to guess what she finds pleasurable. If she expresses her sexual wishes, she may feel guilty. Second, the husband must be aggressive and prove his masculine dominance sexually. This only serves to further repress his wife's sexuality as she becomes afraid of what he might do if she showed any interest at all.

Under these conditions, the sexual sharing of marriage is distorted to a kind of competitive game for two: how long and often can I resist you versus how fast and how often can I have you? Such competition robs sex in marriage of the fellowship of intimacy that God intended (see Genesis 2:24 and its accompanying New Testament passage—1 Corinthians 7; and the Song of Solomon).

The sexual saturation of our society has harmed many marriages by its emphasis on sexual performance. God created sex for expressing intimacy in marriage, not for demonstrating power. "The very emphasis on performance has been the single greatest cause of sexual dysfunction over the ages. . . . Any rigid expectation of a standard of performance is incompatible with good sex" (Gail Sheehy, *Passages,* pp. 441, 452).

Our human frailties show through in every area of life. If we expect perfection of ourselves or our partner, we will not be sensitive to mistakes or open to learn. And everything comes to a screeching halt when we cease to learn and grow.

Sexual Unfaithfulness

One crisis that puts more strain on a marriage than any other is unfaithfulness, particularly if sexual adultery is involved. A recent study showed that "51 percent of our subjects . . . have never cheated . . . thus, remarkably enough, since Kinsey's time there has been no increase in marital infidelity" (Anthony Pietropinto and Jacqueline Simenaur, "Beyond the Male Myth," *Ladies Home Journal,* October 1977, p. 218).

That no increase had been measured in the past 30 years can be viewed with optimism. That 49% of the men responding admitted to being unfaithful, however, should provoke some distress. We dare not think that evangelical Christians are immune, even those who have high standards and are active in the church.

Christians Too?

Over a period of years, a small young church grew to be one of the largest evangelical churches in the entire area. Much of this growth could be attributed to the dedicated energy and personal dynamism of the pastor. He became one of the most influential pastors in his denomination and well known and respected in evangelical circles across the country. His busy schedule of ministry opportunities often took him away from his church and his family. Gradually, his relationship with his wife deteriorated to the point that, though she was a public asset to his church ministry, she couldn't take the pressures and frustrations. Periodically, he would readjust his schedule so he could spend more time with his family, but each time this was done, outside ministry opportunities took the time he had set aside for the family. Lacking deep fellowship with his wife, he took up with another woman whom he felt met some of his emotional and sexual needs. The church asked him to resign.

Only the determination to act responsibly preserved any marriage relationship at all. He made some tough decisions. He confessed publicly to the congregation and sought professional

Christian counseling. His wife's faithfulness and a healing intent on the part of the church leaders made it possible for him to continue in a ministry in another place.

A solution to any marriage crisis requires action. Acting in faith and acting together. If you must act alone, consider the interests of your partner first. This enables God to work in His creative and powerful way.

God Can!

God can heal broken relationships. Housewife Candy Green says, "God gave us back our marriage. Our marriage didn't have a chance in the world. Tom's dream was to become a rock and roll star and mine was to leave my body and join the S-men from Jupiter. . . . Tom and I, each with our own interests and life-styles, drifted farther apart. We began to think of each other's values and hopes as silly and spent our time either fighting or ignoring each other."

They decided to separate. Tom drove Candy to the bus for Washington, D.C. where she was going to "look for God" in an Eastern religious retreat center. As she climbed out of the car, Tom said, "Well, Candy, if you are really looking for God, why don't we do it together?"

"Now, suddenly, we had committed ourselves to a serious search for God. And we had no idea where to begin. . . . We prayed the Lord's Prayer over and over again, six or seven times, then we got up and cleaned the living room. We went to the bedroom, knelt down, said the Lord's Prayer and cleaned the bedroom. We spent the whole day kneeling down, praying the Lord's Prayer and cleaning up rooms.

"At the end of the day we had a nice clean house. And something else happened. We had started the day hating each other; we couldn't even touch each other. But by the end of the day we were holding hands. It was a miracle" (Candy and Tom Green, "God Gave Us Back Our Marriage," *Faith at Work,* October 1977, pp. 5ff). The next day they went to a church service and Candy made a personal decision for Christ. Tom did three months later. Today they are traveling as a singing team sharing that God can make marriage work.

Now this young couple didn't know much. I'm sure someone

could have given them much better advice than repeating the Lord's Prayer interspersed with housecleaning. But God honored their action, commitment, and trust. In their naivete and simplicity they struck the balance of faith and action that allowed God to bring them to Himself and each other.

I can't promise what God will do with your marriage. I do know that you can have a satisfying and growing relationship if you *affirm* God's priorities for you as a couple, *commit* yourselves to work toward these priorities and *trust* God to work in your partner—so you don't have to do it yourself.

9

In Sickness and in Health

The marriage vows include the promise to "have and to hold in sickness and in health," but few healthy young couples have any conception of the stress sickness can bring to a marriage. Perhaps the surprise in this area is that even the common cold can strain marital relationships. Scripture offers a specific plan of action for sickness: "Is anyone among you sick? Let him call for the elders of the church, and let them pray over him, anointing him with oil in the name of the Lord; and the prayer offered in faith will restore the one who is sick, and the Lord will raise him up, and if he has committed sins, they will be forgiven him. Therefore, confess your sins to one another, and pray for one another, so that you may be healed. The effective prayer of a righteous man can accomplish much" (James 5:14-16).

Theologians may debate some of the technicalities of this passage, but I believe it outlines a clear approach to illness. Whether or not you can decide if it promises that all sickness will be healed, to what extent Christians should use medical treatments, or what anointing with oil means, it does tell how to act during a time of sickness. And remember, in the great majority of cases, God wants a person to be well.

The passage lists three actions: call for the elders of the church, pray, and confess your sins. These imply that you should take steps to get well and see a lesson from God for yourself in your sickness.

Death and disease are common throughout Scripture, and their mention shows God's awareness of the human condition. When the disciples asked, "Who sinned, this man or his parents, that he should be born blind?" (John 9:2), they exposed two inadequate understandings of illness by believers. At Jesus' time, apparently, disease was assumed to be a judgment of one's specific sins. Jesus immediately dismissed that explanation. Today, the fallacy seems to be that sin is not taken seriously. Jesus' words are taken almost as a promise of universal cure. However, neither the Bible nor our lives are that simple.

Men of the Bible and Sickness

Job experienced life's monumental crises. His prosperity was taken away, his children killed, and his health broken. His wife complained, "Curse God and die," and his friends criticized rather than comforted. Job did not receive God's thanks or congratulations for what he had endured. Instead, God confronted Job with His powerful presence and Job concluded, "I have declared that which I did not understand, things too wonderful for me, which I did not know. Hear, now and I will speak; I will ask Thee, and do Thou instruct me. I have heard of Thee by the hearing of the ear; but now my eye sees Thee; Therefore I retract, and I repent in dust and ashes" (Job 42:3-6). Though Job had remained righteous in deed and steadfastly refused to surrender his faith, he had not affirmed God's plan for him, which was beyond his understanding. God was teaching Job, and us, that His purpose cannot always be understood.

God confronted Nebuchadnezzar similarly with mental illness. Even after being warned in a dream interpreted by Daniel (Dan. 4:5-27), Nebuchadnezzar said, "Is this not Babylon the great, which I myself have built as a royal residence by the might of my power and for the glory of my majesty?" (Dan. 4:30) Immediately, he was stricken with an insanity that caused him to live as a senseless animal (Dan. 4:33). But he learned what God was teaching him and concluded, "Now I, Nebuchadnezzar, praise, exalt, and honor the King of heaven, for all His works are true and His ways just, and He is able to humble those who walk in pride" (Dan. 4:37). What a contrast!

In the New Testament as well, God used a health problem to stimulate humility and an understanding of His own greatness and purpose. Many have speculated and debated over the identity of Paul's "thorn in the flesh," but Paul himself leaves no doubt about its purpose when he wrote: "To keep me from exalting myself, there was given me a thorn in the flesh, a messenger of Satan to buffet me . . . Concerning this I entreated the Lord three times that it might depart from me. And He has said to me, 'My grace is sufficient for you, for power is perfected in weakness.' Most gladly, therefore, I will rather boast about my weakness, that the power of Christ may dwell in me. Therefore I am well content with weaknesses, with insults, with distresses, with persecutions, with difficulties for Christ's sake; for when I am weak, then I am strong" (2 Cor. 12:7-10).

Job and Paul are giants of Scripture. Their diseases served to humble them before God. Sickness was the avenue for catching a vision of God's purposes for them. The same can be true for us today. Look for God when you are sick. He meets you at your point of need. Even the common cold can be an opportunity for a new look to God.

Minor Sicknesses

Minor sicknesses can be very humbling. A friend of mine had a sore throat one summer and kept on working. It developed into a bad case of strep throat. More than a week went by before he could function normally. He remarked afterward that he didn't understand how just a sore throat could debilitate him so badly for so long. His "important" work waited nicely until he fully recovered.

To be humbled by a "little cold" or "just a sore throat" is hard for many people to cope with, especially men who feel they can conquer the world by sheer strength. Dean Merrill, author of *The Husband Book,* comments: "Factors such as these lead women to say that men don't cope well with sickness, are 'big babies,' etc. They're often correct. Part of it definitely has to do with our efficiency mind-set. But another part has to do with the traditional masculine self-image of toughness and independence. Many of us can't stand to be weak or vulnerable. So when sickness does precisely that to us, we turn cranky. We know we don't look like big, strong he-men any more, and that makes us mad. Our ego has been bruised" (Dean Merrill, *The Husband Book,* Grand Rapids: Zondervan, 1977, p. 166).

Merrill also points out that your attitude toward sickness has a lot to do with how you respond to it. If a husband and wife take different approaches, they can end up with a serious conflict on their hands. He admits that he and his wife "have a good deal of adjusting in this area, since I tend to underplay sickness and she tends to overplay it. When I was growing up, we seldom went to the doctor; the assumption was that the less spotlight given to illness, the less it would be around. In her family, health discussions seemed to get more air time.

"So we've had more than one disagreement about what to call various sets of symptoms. We haven't completely resolved the problem yet, but we're working on it. On two or three different occasions I've brushed off a baby's crying in the night as simply teething or bad dreams; finally, Grace has persuaded me that it ought to be checked by the pediatrician, and it has turned out to be an ear infection that definitely needed medication" (Dean Merrill, *The Husband Book,* pp. 167-168).

Chronic Health Problems

Many people face chronic health problems that are not totally debilitating, but require regular attention. Various kinds of diabetes, epilepsy, multiple sclerosis, and arthritis fall into this category, as do certain physical handicaps. The treatments, doctor's visits, and limitations become part of life's routine but the effects are real. In some cases, slow deterioration is evident; in others, the possibility of a rapid worsening exists. Sometimes the needed medications must be handled with extreme caution and are often a hated nuisance.

One of the men who works with me has observed this problem with his mother who was diagnosed as having rheumatoid arthritis when he was a young teen. He recalls the variety of treatments that became the norm in his home. Strong drugs, painful exercises, and self-administered injections were common. Everyone was expected to do more work to help Mother with the house. All concepts of "male" and "female" jobs were abandoned in the interest of getting them done. Life was different and sometimes difficult for the family, but it did not stop. Through it all the children learned to help, to be sensitive to suffering, and to be more understanding of other people's needs and problems.

IN SICKNESS AND IN HEALTH / 99

Response to Sickness

Children learn how to respond to illness by observing how their parents respond when they are sick. So if you will act positively at times of illness, your children will be better able to cope with their own sicknesses as well as with the times you are ill. Children need examples of how to cope with problems and stress, which you can give them in such times.

Though sickness is a result of sin, not every specific sickness comes from a specific sin. Sickness is universal. *Affirm* that God has a positive purpose in your sickness. Perhaps it is something for you to learn or a sin for you to confess. Possibly, this illness gives an opportunity for service or witness that you wouldn't have any other way. Even if God's purposes are hidden from you, continue to affirm that He has a constructive plan that includes you. This affirmation does not mean that you can't ask questions or admit your doubts. Particularly in cases of catastrophes, questions and doubts are an important part of the coping and healing process.

Commit yourself to take some action. In our society, this is probably assumed to be seeking medical attention. I certainly wouldn't rule that out, but I think Christians have another whole dimension to their resources. James suggested three specific things to do: call for the elders, pray, and confess.

No believer should have to face a medical crisis alone. God has given the church to His children for just such an occasion. This is not just an abstract and theological concept of community. This is gutsy involvement in each other's lives. In the book about his daughter's near-fatal automobile accident, Roy Zuck, of Dallas Seminary, tells how involved people in their church became in the vigil over Barb's broken and unconscious body:

"Bill is an elder at the church where we are members. Somehow he heard about our situation and he came to the hospital to explain his solution. 'The elders want to sit with Barb during the evenings and nights. This will relieve you from having to pay private-duty nurses.'

"And what a relief it was! Bill's offer was most welcome. He set up a schedule of three-hour shifts for the elders and others to sit with Barb. Dottie and I were deeply touched by their sacrifice" (Roy Zuck, *Barb, Please Wake Up!* Wheaton: Victor Books, 1976, p. 43).

The Church and Sickness

James wrote that your elders shouldn't "somehow hear" of your need; you should send for them. People with needs often suffer needlessly because they have not told anyone from their church of their problem. They then feel a simmering anger toward those who don't come to help. All that's needed is to ask. Asking is a sign of faith and releases any pent-up anger. It is the beginning of the healing process.

Years ago I had a serious problem with my back. After strenuous exertion and with excruciating pain, I left for a short speaking ministry in Wyoming. Each day the situation worsened and the pain increased. I was bent over as I walked; I slept on the floor and felt no relief from treatments I received.

One day the Lord reminded me of the command in James to call for the elders of the church, and rebuked me for my unbelief. My heart was broken as the Lord gently showed me how I had tried everything but His method and that I really didn't trust Him and obey His word at this point. I wept as I thought of how much I had grieved God and promised Him I would do it before the day passed. I also promised I would confess my grieving the Lord to the people at the church that night and ask the elders to pray for me even though the congregation was not accustomed to that practice.

After the meeting, we met in the pastor's home and the elders, totally ignorant of the Scripture in James 5, asked that I explain it to them. We all confessed our sins, especially that of not obeying God's Word. They anointed me with some mineral oil and we prayed for God's healing. One elder then said, "What are we to expect now? Are you going to straighten up and be completely healed?"

"I don't know." I said, "We have obeyed the Lord, and that is the least we can do and the most we can do."

That night, with the same pain and crippledness, I crawled into my sleeping bag on the floor, since a soft bed would have aggravated the problem. The next morning I woke up a new man—no pain or stiffness. I was healed. I jumped up and down in joy and thanksgiving.

Prayer has become our last resort rather than our first thought. When James says to call for the elders, we begin to get a little shaky. But when he says to confess our sins to each other, we are positively petrified. Now if there was ever a high-risk commitment, that's it! Yet as we've seen, pride in one form or another was at the root of the sickness of Job, Nebuchadnezzar, Paul, and my own. Confessing your sins out loud to another Christian really shoots down that pride and opens us up to God's healing in our emotions.

Another commitment that parents need to make, in the health area, is to prepare their children to receive health care before they need it. Taking your child with you when you go to the doctor or dentist will make his visits there more predictable. Don't lie about the possibilities of pain, but let him know that it can be managed for his own good. Your own response to injections and other painful treatments will be a good model for your child in this area. When your child is to be the patient, go over in advance just what he can expect. This is particularly important if a hospital visit is in the offing. Surgery for your child should be discussed thoroughly in advance. Don't stimulate unnecessary fears, but be honest. If the child is prepared and can say to himself, "Yes, this is what Dad told me would happen," he will cope with it much better than if it is a total surprise.

Often, parents can trust God for themselves more easily than they can their children. It is almost universal for parents to wish they could trade places with their suffering children. What is needed instead is for their trust in God to be so evident to their children that they will have the confidence to trust Him too. That sort of trust may be the greatest strength and weapon against fear a suffering child can have.

Menstruation

Before I move on to consider some specific health crises, I think I should discuss a common health issue that every family must face. I hesitate to call it a problem, for it is only a problem if you let it be. It is a woman's monthly cycle, menstruation. It is an area where a husband's action can make a big difference for his wife and the rest of the family.

Dean Merrill suggests: "We keep forgetting, even though we've been told all the medical facts, how the hormone levels rise and fall to create fretfulness and depression at certain times of the month. We hear phrases like, 'There's just no way for you to know what this is like'—and she's right. There isn't.

"But we can learn how to make life easier for her. Whether it's fixing our own breakfast so she can sleep in, giving back rubs, or postponing our remarks about the state of the checking account, we can do a lot to accommodate the monthly period, especially in the first couple of days" (Merrill, *The Husband Book,* p. 139).

Attitude will make a big difference, perhaps not in the physical symptoms but in how they affect the whole family. First, keep in mind that menstruation is a natural, normal process. It is part of God's plan and can be affirmed as His unique design. To call it "the curse" or "the sickness" censures God's plan and creates unnecessary stress. This is very important for both husband and wife to understand. Furthermore, it is important to teach children, both boys and girls, about menstruation in a positive, natural fashion. Another thing that is very important is to recognize that not all women experience the same things with their menstrual cycles. In one small Bible study group, the couples, becoming close friends, were aware when one of the women was having her period. The women then discovered that their symptoms were all different, and realized how this was a unique problem for each one. The awareness of these differences helped each woman come to a new appreciation of herself and be better able to cope.

A damaging and persistent concept is that women are helpless captives of irrational emotions during their periods. Many women and men believe this and find themselves responding as though it were true, making for a kind of self-fulfilling prophecy. Certainly, there can be some practical changes of which both husbands and wives should be aware. A placid person can become irritable; her sense of humor may wane and she may lose perspective. She may become exceptionally talkative and find it hard to concentrate. Sometimes she may have difficulty making decisions and become forgetful. Though fatigue is one of the worst problems during these days, she may suddenly become abnormally active. If a woman knows what to expect during the different phases of her cycle and learns to adapt herself to them, she has the key to her own personality. A husband who understands and accepts these different phases will be able to reinforce and assist his wife intelligently and affectionately.

To escape the crises that this can bring on a couple requires a commitment to be well informed and supportive. It is a team effort and relational problems during this monthly period can be minimized with constructive action. A husband who sees his wife's periods as evidence of her weakness, contributes to her monthly suffering. On the other hand, a supportive husband can make life much more pleasant for both himself and his wife. Even the children should become part of the process of helping Mom with her monthly periods. As girls mature, their cycles should be taken into account in the family routine.

Victory over Tragedy

The Act principle can be a significant help through the everyday sorts of health problems we face. When a major health crisis descends on you, however, these principles are essential, and you will need God, your church, and your faith. Your ability to *affirm* God's leading may become clouded; your ability to *commit* yourself to specific action may weaken; you may be left only with *trusting* God for something you don't know, understand, or expect. Survival may overshadow recovery. Bills may mount to create a financial crisis as well. Relationships will be altered and strain your marriage. Romans 8:28 may become almost a mockery in your ears, yet it is God's Word: "We know that God causes all things to work together for good to those who love God, to those who are called according to His purpose."

This is why it is so necessary that during more normal days, preparation is made for an unforeseen crisis. The act of committing your body to God ahead of time, during health, will make the affirmation and trust easier and more natural during the dark days.

Victory is possible even in the face of medical failure. A lovely young mother of two had been a childhood diabetic and she became blind.

She determined to be cheerful and not infect others with her times of depression. She has established a small circle of Christian friends with whom she can share her down times without dragging them down too. She allows them to take her shopping or to lunch as therapy for her cooped-up feelings.

She has established new household routines that allow her

children and husband to be around when she is doing tasks that require vision. She has become adept at reading and writing in braille and collects recipes for dishes she can prepare without visual judgment.

Rather than becoming angry with God, this has been a time of great spiritual growth for the entire family. They have questions, but they recognize God's grace and find spiritual resources in a small Bible study group and their prayer for each other. This young mother acted positively in the face of crisis, and her husband, whose spirituality had been minimal, began to hunger for spiritual growth and fellowship.

What Happened to Barbara?

I have already mentioned Barbara Zuck and her father's book describing her accident and recovery. By giving us this window on their experience, the Zucks offered much help to others who face health crises. They revealed the questions they asked, the real benefits from their ordeal, and what help came from other people.

The questions they asked were crucial and came when they were least able to think clearly and make good decisions. Every decision became an act of faith. "How will her mental abilities be affected?" they asked. "Would she be permanently paralyzed in some way? Will she be in a vegetative state for the rest of her life? Lord, how long and why this terrible ordeal? Why should this problem have to continue? What was the Lord trying to tell us?

"Like giant rats, those questions began to gnaw at my mind. But I kept them to myself, not wanting to add to Dottie's fear. And yet I realized she was probably thinking similar questions" (Zuck, *Barb, Please Wake Up!* pp. 86, 16).

To verbalize horrible questions is devastating, but not to talk them over together is torture. At such a time, husband and wife can easily become isolated from each other, immersed in their private griefs. But those griefs should not be private. A commitment to talk them through, to cry and pray together may keep you working together through a crisis, but it must be a mutual commitment, because it will not be comfortable for either of you. Asking questions is necessary, even if we do not have satisfying answers. The friend who can encourage and accept these questions without giving pat answers performs a great ministry.

From their questions, the Zucks found a way to pray that brought together both their trust in God and their submission to His will. "Our prayers could not tell God what to do. They had to be voiced in an attitude of willing submission to His best plan for our lives. I believe I was honest when I prayed, 'Lord, if You will receive glory to Yourself by Barb being a cripple in a wheelchair or a vegetable the remainder of her life, then that is what we want. On the other hand, if it is Your desire to restore her, we will glorify You for that' " (Zuck, *Barb, Please Wake Up!* p. 45).

Yet, their awareness of God's presence, peace, and power did not automatically dispel the sorrow and physical exhaustion. This suggests to me that trust and grief can go together, and while a Christian is grieving he can also experience God's comfort. We "sorrow not, even as others who have no hope" (1 Thes. 4:13, KJV)—yet we sorrow.

Shared Crisis

To survive a crisis like the Zucks', it must be shared between husband and wife. But the medical crisis can prompt personal and marital stress that compounds the whole problem. Dottie's physical strength was sapped and her emotional health shattered. She woke up morning after morning crying and Roy felt he had a second patient to care for. He tried to encourage her by their spending time together, going on walks, and by his helping with the housework. He kept a diary and they consoled each other by comparing each day's progress. Statistics show that a tragic number of divorces occur after a child's serious illness if special attention is not given to the marriage relationship during the crisis.

What good came from Barb's accident and pain and the suffering of her family? One was the opportunity to tell others about Jesus Christ. As Barb was leaving the hospital, she remarked, "I don't know if anyone has become a Christian through this or not, but if even one person were to accept the Lord I would go through this 50 times." As of this writing, they know of three. Through the outreach of the book there are probably others.

One of the other benefits of this experience for Roy Zuck was a "deepening of my ability to 'weep with them that weep' (Rom. 12:15, KJV). Never before had I known the heavy feeling of parents whose child is injured, faces surgery, or is dying. Now I knew. Now I could reach out to others and say, 'I understand how you feel.' "

The Zucks were amazed at what other Christians did for them during their time of crisis. The lesson they learned could well be learned by all Christians. Of the people who stayed with them through Barb's first surgery Roy wrote, "Their presence expressed their Christian love, and we were greatly strengthened by their concern. I had to confess to the Lord that I had never done that for anyone. Now that I knew how much it meant, I would seek to share the blessing in the future."

You may not have to face such a crisis, but if you are in fellow-ship with God's people, you will be in touch with hurting people whom you can comfort. You can commit yourself to be available in specific ways. The Zucks offer suggestions of things that were helpful to them, and a few things to avoid that were difficult for them, though people were well-meaning.

"Send cards with notes to the patient and/or his loved ones. . . . A card which included a handwritten note of comfort and encour-agement was . . . uplifting. Notice I wrote 'cards' plural.

"Telephone the injured person's loved ones. Though some people might not care to answer the phone frequently, I found that inquiries by telephone were encouraging. Sometimes it was easier to talk with them over the phone than in person.

"Visit the patient or his loved ones at the hospital. . Though a patient appears unconscious he may be able to hear and remember what is said. The presence of friends was especially supportive during the long surgeries.

"Be prayerful about what you say. To us, the presence, not the sage counsel, of visitors was the most meaningful. They chatted with us about various subjects, helping to pass the time. We sensed little value in attempts to 'theologize' about the purpose for this trial. . . . If someone said to us, 'I understand,' we doubted that he really did . . . But his saying 'I'm so sorry,' or 'I've been praying for you,' was definitely more comforting. One well-intentioned person caused grief rather than uplift by mention-ing a relative who had died at about Barb's age. . . . Another comment that sliced like a knife into my wife's heart was a ques-tion by people who did not know our family well: 'Do you have other children?' . . . To Dottie it implied: . . . 'Do you have other children to compensate for this loss?' The question would be better if it were pointed clearly to the other children: 'Tell me about the rest of your family.'

"Help in tangible ways. Many people said, 'Let me know if I can help.' They meant well, of course, but of greater help were those who offered specific assistance. One example: 'We want to bring you your supper. Would tomorrow night or the next night be better?' Preparing a meal for the family of a hospital patient may not seem to be much help, but it is a highly appreciated load carrier. Picking up the dishes afterward or using disposable dishes avoids the addition of one more chore.

"Ask what specific needs you can pray for. Knowing that people were interceding for Barb's particular needs was more encouraging to us than general prayer support. And God answered in response to specific prayer burdens. For example, not long after several people prayed for Barb's left eye, it began to open. Others, after praying for her left arm, were thrilled to see her move it. Prayers by God's people recorded in the Bible were specific. Ours should be too" (Zuck, *Barb, Please Wake Up,* p. 87).

10

Middlescence

The expression, "mid-life crisis" has been popularized, more than any one thing, by *Passages*. The mid-life crisis, of all of the crises I have discussed in this book, has the greatest opportunity for bringing constructive change to your life or destruction and hopelessness. It will become the old age of youth or the youth of old age. When secular people act responsibly, they find that life moves more constructively. I believe, however, that Christians have unique resources for facing the mid-life crises that are unknown outside the family of God.

Though talking about having a mid-life crisis is now fashionable, the experience of it is certainly not new. Author Joe Bayly observes, "The mid-life crisis is not some new discovery by our super-brilliant American psychologists. Saul went through it. So did David. And Solomon. They make good case studies" (Joseph Bayly, "The Me Generation," *Eternity*, October 1977, p. 81).

The "destruction that wasteth at noonday" is a phrase from Psalm 91 that effectively describes (though that is not its biblical intention) the feelings that plague people at this time of their lives. This psalm is a powerful promise of God's care and protection that the believer can claim:

> He that dwelleth in the secret place of the Most High shall abide under the shadow of the Almighty. I will say of the Lord, He is my refuge and my fortress: my God; in Him will I trust. Surely He shall deliver thee from the snare of the fowler, and from the noisome pestilence. He shall cover thee with His feathers, and under His wings shalt thou trust: His truth shall

be thy shield and buckler. Thou shalt not be afraid for the terror by night: nor for the arrow that flieth by day; nor for the pestilence that walketh in darkness; nor for the destruction that wasteth at noonday (Ps. 91:1-6, KJV).

Mid-Life and Middle Age

Our language can be confusing when we talk about mid-life and middle age, for they are not the same. Mid-life is a time of upheaval, uncertainty, and questioning. Middle age, on the other hand, is marked by growth, stability, serenity, and satisfaction. For many, the questions of adolescence that they thought were settled, rear their confusing heads again. Interestingly, this frequently coincides with the adolescence of their children. So perhaps one reason many parents have difficulty helping their teenage children with their questions, is that they are unable to answer the same questions for themselves. But by middle age, they have found a more relaxed life-stance and can enjoy their grandchildren.

Though the term "mid-life" appears to be mathematically derived (35 is half of the life expectancy of 70), its onset is not mathematically predictable. The internal life-clock is paced by a variety of outward elements: age at marriage and age of spouse, age and number of children, career history. "Working-class men describe themselves as middle-aged at 40 and old by 60. Business executives and professionals, by contrast, do not see themselves as reaching middle age until 50, and old age means 70 to them" (Sheehy, *Passages,* p. 375).

The passing of time and an awareness of aging are at the core of the mid-life crisis. The youthful sense of limitless, infinite time vanishes. The central question is, *What am I going to do with the rest of my life?*

Men and women seem to respond in almost opposite ways to that question. For men and career women, the time is compressed to an urgency to do something significant before it is too late. Sheehy characterized the attitude of the mid-life men and career women this way: " 'Time is running out. Time must be beaten. Can I accomplish all that I'd hoped before it's too late?' To women who have been at home, time is suddenly seen as long: 'Look at all the time ahead! After the children are gone, what will I do with it?' " (Sheehy, *Passages,* p. 353)

Like many other predictable crises of life, this one passes. The questions and doubts of mid-life may seem trivial or even juvenile from the perspective of middle age, but at the time they are being experienced, they are real and intense. It hardly seems possible that what is so distressing and perplexing today will be a chuckle of private embarrassment in a few years. For this reason, you need to prepare to act when these difficult days come, and not be swept away in their confusing eddies and crosscurrents.

The Brevity of Life

The Psalms again offer a perspective on the passage of life and the priorities of its brevity. Moses spoke from the security of the Lord's "dwelling place in all generations" when he wrote of life's frustrating briefness (Ps. 90:9-12, KJV):

For all our days are passed away in Thy wrath: we spend our years as a tale that is told. The days of our years are three-score years and ten; and if by reason of strength they be fourscore years, yet is their strength labor and sorrow; for it is soon cut off, and we fly away. Who knoweth the power of Thine anger? even according to Thy fear, so is Thy wrath. So teach us to number our days, that we may apply our hearts to wisdom.

Death is the inexorable, inescapable limit to human dreams. Most people have half of their lives ahead of them at the mid-life crossing, but are aware of the final deadline creeping closer. Their own death becomes a reality for the first time and more of life seems behind them than ahead of them.

A specific death may bring this realization. Perhaps the first of their parents or their spouse's parents dies. The grief of that is enough, but if they subtract their age from that of the deceased, they recognize the limited time that is left. When the last of these parents is gone, the blow can be even greater. They have fully "come-of-age" and become the senior generation.

If the deaths of parents is the frontal attack, the deaths of friends is the sneak attack from the flank. People are unprepared for facing the mortality of those their same age. When my friend, Paul Little, of Inter-Varsity died in an accident, I was stunned. He was younger than I and I began to feel my days were numbered. Even a close call can leave someone gasping, "That could have been me!" Death will be discussed in the last chapter, but needs some attention here as the mainspring of the life-clock that pushes a crisis upon you.

A Turning Point

More than any other crisis, mid-life fulfills the definition of a crisis, drawn from Erik Erikson, in chapter 1, "Not a catastrophe, but a turning point, a crucial period of increasing vulnerability and heightened potential." It is a time of reevaluating dreams and goals. Whether or not the first half of your life has seen your dreams come true, you are vulnerable at mid-life. How well I know the struggle!

On the surface, those who have succeeded early in their careers may not seem susceptible to the disillusionment that comes at mid-life. However, without a new goal and a new reason to expend energy, the rest of life becomes hollow. Especially dangerous are careers built on youth, accompanied by a great deal of public recognition. Many professional athletes, entertainers, and entrepreneurs have had difficulty finding a suitable goal to follow early success, and their later lives have been wasted. Alexander the Great is reported to have wept as a young man that there were no more worlds to conquer.

Some who have seemingly done it all before 30 have launched into new endeavors to find even greater fulfillment. Charles Percy had become president of Bell and Howell before he was 30. He is credited with turning a sagging company into a profitable success. Where could he go when he was already on top of the corporate heap? He turned to public service and has been an active and renowned U.S. Senator.

More common, though, is the person whose dreams have not been fulfilled by age 35. Few people are able to reach their secret goals. If this is your situation, as is quite likely, you may feel that your life has been wasted. You may doubt your competence and question whether you have found your place in the world. You may give up believing that your dream was ever possible, valid, or worthy.

If these feelings take their natural course, you will dig yourself into despair. You will lose your sense of self-respect and ask how you could have been so foolish as to think you could realize your dream. You may even feel guilty that you committed yourself to such an illusory goal. And, perhaps worst of all, you may feel guilty that you sold out your dream, your ideals, your very self to get ahead when getting ahead turned out to be an empty prize.

As these emotions sweep down on you, you may discover a whole emotional dimension of your inner self. This can be an emotion-laden time of life which may catch you by surprise. Men, particularly, are alarmed at the emotions that emerge. If you let these emotions determine the course of the crisis, you will find only disappointment. You can, however, discover a new meaning and fulfillment in life if you act to guide your journey through the transition.

I remember the trauma and confusion of my mid-life experience. I had traveled for years in a God-blessed ministry and had had more opportunities than I could say grace over. Outwardly, there was no reason to feel restless, but I could not go on, even though many new avenues of ministry were open to me. Early every morning I drove to a park to meditate and pray. I had an empty feeling that I was on the sidelines and the whole work of God would go by me. I longed to be in the harvest field and made a new commitment to God and whatever He wanted. God graciously helped me. The new vision, positive emotions, and clear guidance that emerged from this crisis thrust me into the greatest opportunity of my life.

The potential for disaster, however, is real and significant. When you begin to feel you have the experience anad maturity to give others guidance, particularly your teenage children, you lose your own sense of direction. But the opportunity for a renewed and more realistic vision, a more focused and genuine contribution is also great. A serious self-evaluation is necessary, with possible alterations in your course of action.

If your priorities have put family and church ahead of your job, you will find that getting satisfaction through serving will be much easier than if career success has been your consuming life goal.

Self-Evaluation

To undergo a systematic self-evaluation at mid-life may be threatening. It may seem like a return to your high school or college career guidance counselor. Yet it is the most wholesome act of faith you can take at this time. It *affirms* you still believe God has something for you. He does, and you can find it. You might try reading up on some great people who have achieved some of their most significant accomplishments in the second half of their lives: C. S. Lewis, Corrie ten Boom, T. S. Eliot, Albert Einstein, Paul Tournier, Igor Stravinsky, Ethel Waters, Margaret Mead, Norman Rockwell, Malcolm Muggeridge, Katherine Hepburn, Pablo Picasso, and Thomas Edison.

To do the evaluation requires *commitment*, but the commitment that really counts is to change your life pattern in response to what you learn. As frustrating as the career you have now may be, it is a security. The risk of starting over is frightening. However, it is a risk you can take if you *trust* God with the outcome of your life.

Changing Relationships

Relationships change with time even more than careers, for they are dynamic and constantly readjusted. Several primary relationships shift noticeably at mid-life and need to be renegotiated. Your relationship with your spouse is of first importance, followed by your relationship with your children. Your parents alter their relationship to you at this time; there is a shift in your friendships.

You will encounter a great deal of tension and stress if you allow your relationships to drift through this period. Social pressures will pull against your intentions.

Consider marriage: even among Christians, divorce seems to be considered an avenue for making this adjustment in the marriage relationship. But to take that approach is to treat the marriage *commitment* too lightly. The commitment is permanent and within this permanence you can *affirm* that God has drawn you together and can guide you through the remainder of your lives. You can *trust* Him to make each of you a support to the other, rather than an unbearable burden.

For example, contrast two husbands Joe Bayly describes: "I heard of a man whose wife was diagnosed as having cancer. His first reaction? 'I'll divorce her.' . . . I knew another man whose wife was totally incapacitated by a stroke. For nine years, until he himself was struck down, he took care of her total needs. After that long period, she had no bedsore. Two weeks after she was put in a nursing home, she developed them; another two weeks, and she died" (Bayly, "The Me Generation," *Eternity*, p. 81).

If you are committed to each other, you can face the prospect of changing together. The alternative is drifting apart. You can trust God to give you a common ground of marital fellowship even when you discover differences you never knew you had. Then you can courageously embark on an open evaluation of your marriage which is the only way to bring new vitality into your mid-life relationship. The alternative is deadly boredom.

This evaluation process can easily degenerate into a struggle between you if there is not a positive attitude. The natural human tendency is to fix blame on the other. Rather than seeing a shared responsibility to work on the relationship, each tries to blame the other for not only the marriage troubles but all of the problems of this mid-life muddle—the restlessness, heightened emotional needs, and changing roles.

Seeking Professional Help
Often, "the two people go round and round the accusation tree until one of them says, 'You really need some help. I think you should see a psychiatrist or a marriage counselor.' The trouble with this suggestion is the motive. What the mate usually wants is a judgment that the other is the guilty party. Sensing this, the partner who has been told to go to a psychiatrist often digs in his or her heels and refuses because to set foot inside this arbiter's office would be an admission that 'I'm the sick one' " (Sheehy, *Passages*, p. 375).

I know I've said it before, but it is so important I must say it again. Seek help if you get to the place where you are not making progress on your own. This is much wiser than fighting your way through and permanently damaging your relationship. Your pastor is probably the best person to start with. A responsible pastor will soon detect if your problem is beyond his ability to help and will send you to another professional. This move can usually only be made as a joint effort: share the problem together and seek help together.

If you feel that outside help is needed, but your partner refuses to go, swallow your pride and go by yourself. You will thus assume responsibility for your share of the problem and your share of the solution. I've often seen a stalemate broken when a partner steps out of the accusing role and puts himself in the help-seeking role. The conventional defenses of an uncooperative partner are turned around. Whatever you do, don't use this as a new weapon on your spouse or seek for vindication of your position. Honestly ask God to enable the counselor to give you the understanding you need. In this way, you can commit yourself to positive action as a start toward improving the relationship. You are the key in this situation.

The mid-life crisis could be described as the "death-throes" of adolescence. It is a necessary upheaval and rethinking before the maturity of middle age. You may look to your parents, as you did when you were an adolescent, but may be shocked at how little they can help. One or both of your parents may have died, or may be weakening physically and lacking the wisdom you need for coping with your world. They may even be looking to you to be their caretaker, reversing the parent-child role.

Career Changes

Constructive action on the career front can help you resolve other mid-life issues. It can give you a stable base from which to re-establish relationships with your spouse, your children, and your parents. A diligent reevaluation of your life priorities, giving success a proper place behind spiritual and family relationships, will make a career change less distressing. Your new career direction may even bring growth to these relationships rather than additional frustration and discord.

Working through career uncertainty can give you a whole new lease on life and does not necessarily mean you must change jobs.

One couple lived their whole lives in the upper Midwest. The husband had grown restless and when their last child was married they both felt free to move. Financial responsibilities were minimal, with only two of them, and the risks of moving manageable. They sold their home and with great expectations moved to the Southwest. But what had been a winter escape from snow became an oven in the summer. They found it difficult to establish strong relationships in a new church and the new job was not as ideal as had been expected. They decided to return to their old hometown and lived in an apartment till they could find a suitable home to purchase. The experiment was costly and unpleasant, but they learned. They could never have been satisfied with the old town, the old job, and the old church, had they not made the pilgrimage. The risk of action was necessary to know the direction for the future.

Another couple made a similar move when the last child was married, which precipitated several years of disorientation before finding a new niche. They had lived in the same house for 20 years, the husband had always worked for the same company, and they attended the same church for 30 years.

He quit that job and took another in an entirely different field, though they stayed in the same area. That proved unsatisfactory, so they explored other possibilities. The direction of their church began to change and they felt rootless and disappointed. Finally, they moved to another city and struggled through several other disappointments. It was a tough time of change and adjustment, but they are now both settled in satisfying jobs in two Christian organizations with a sense of ministry they never had before.

A transition may be forced on us rather than voluntarily chosen. This may be God's way of directing us to the future. Two friends of mine—a married couple—experienced this. They both lost good jobs at about the same time. What could have caused panic became an opportunity. They took over a gas and grocery operation in a booming suburb, and are running the business together. They have a closer relationship than ever before because they feel the pressure of the business drawing them together. In spite of the expected difficulties, both marriage and business are now thriving.

These three couples took different paths through the mid-life crisis. Yet they shared in common the *commitment* to take action that implied risk. In each case they faced difficulty. The first couple found the difficulty to be an *affirmation* of their previous life-style. The second persevered through the difficulty to find a new fulfillment in ministry jobs for both husband and wife. The third couple discovered that the difficulties of starting a new business drew them together and helped develop their marriage relationship more fully. In every case, they had to *do* something to know if they were on the right track. They had to *trust* God with the risk of their futures. They did not give up when the emotions and disruptions of mid-life surprised them and derailed what they had assumed would always be stable.

The crises brought them to the youth of old age and they started over with new vision, vigor, and victory.

11

Your Graying Years

American culture has always had something of a youth orientation. The postwar baby boom made it a highly profitable obsession and growing old became the ultimate social sin. The lowered status that comes with increasing age was covered over with terms like "senior citizens" and "golden years." The Bible is more honest, and with this honesty comes a dignity and respect that is missing in our culture. God's care is promised through the graying years (Isa. 46:4).

Media observers, reporting a shifting trend, are now starting to talk about "the graying of America." The "war babies" are approaching middle age. The same group who made the youth culture big a few years ago will emphasize the questions of aging in the next few years. They are a large group with latent political and economic power.

Some groups, such as the Gray Panthers, are already raising questions that will become burning issues in American society during the next few years. Some of those questions will be addressed on a personal level in this chapter. For instance, how can you build a meaningful marriage when your children are grown and on their own? How can you prepare for retirement? How can you make the best use of your retirement years? How can you grow old gracefully?

After the Empty Nest
Your children may prompt in you an awareness of your own aging as they become more independent and more adult. Women,

118

particularly, who have not worked as their children grew up begin to fear what has been called the "empty nest." It is interesting that the fear of the empty nest is so negative when the experience for many turns out to be so positive. For many women, menopause arrives just as the children are getting ready to leave. The loss of the mothering role can be quite a shock, but once a woman knows she will never have another child, a new kind of creativity is released. She is free to give herself to larger social concerns, spiritual ministries, and meaningful activities.

I was talking with Dr. Ted Engstrom of World Vision. He had just spent some time discussing the problems of the empty nest with 70 Christian couples at a retreat. He said, "I was amazed at how acute this problem is with so many." Though their children are gone, Ted and Dorothy are so involved with significant ministries that they don't have time for self-pity and loneliness.

The solution to the empty nest is so simple: be active. When the empty nest materializes, most couples find they have plenty to do. This period can be one of the most satisfying and rewarding periods of life.

New Growth Potential

When the children leave, you have a great opportunity and potential for new growth in your relationship with each other. You may discover, however, that you have drifted apart over the years of child-rearing, and have poured your lives into your children instead of your marriage. This is the real tragedy of the empty nest and it emphasizes the fact that a couple's marriage should have a higher priority than their children. Marriage is permanent, but parenthood is temporary.

Howard Hendricks tells of a woman who was distressed at the thought of her son going away to college. "I'm going to be so lonely. I'll feel so useless," she cried. "Can you help me?" Howard asked her, "What have you been trying to accomplish as his mother all these years? What has been your goal as a mother?" To which she answered, "To get him ready for college." Howard then responded, "Why, woman, you've succeeded! You should be singing the Hallelujah Chorus. He's doing just what you've been preparing him for for eighteen years."

Jesus said, "A man shall leave his father and mother" (Mark

10:7). Successful parenthood is preparing your children to leave you. If your goal has been to raise your children to mature, responsible adulthood, you can rejoice when they become independent enough to care for themselves. You will probably find it a relief and a help to your marriage when they are old enough to be on their own.

One young woman, the oldest of several children, is leaving for college feeling somewhat insecure. Though she has resisted some parental discipline at home, she is a bit frightened that it will be absent. She will be on her own. Emptying the nest is more of a trauma for her than the parents. They are anxious for the contest of wills to end. They are ready to relate to her as an independent adult, glad to relinquish the direct, daily strings of authority.

Starting Over as a Couple

One couple found a new lease on life with the emptying of the nest. When their children were growing up, they took them everywhere. Whatever they did, their children did with them. Now the kids are married and for the first time these parents can be alone. They can take their vacations and go where they want to unhindered, and it's great. The husband is retired, but works when it's possible. His wife is younger, and works when she can. They are enjoying again the same kind of freedom they had when they were first married.

Current family research strongly supports the fact that most couples find the emptying of the nest to be a positive, fresh beginning of a new stage in life. One study makes the point so well that I want to share some of its practical insights.

Irwin Deutscher noted that "most parents are gradually prepared to some degree for the day when their children marry and leave home by their periodic absences away at school or elsewhere." In fact, this process starts earlier than most people seem to think. Of the parents studied, "Nearly a quarter of the families interviewed had parted with their children for extended periods of time while they were still in their teens" (Irwin Deutscher, "Socialization for Postparental Life," *Family Roles and Interaction: An Anthology,* Jerold Heiss, ed., Chicago: Rand McNally, 1976, pp. 427).

I suspect even those first weeks at summer camp during the

preteen years may start this process. Many high school young people devote their summers to jobs, camps, and missionary service away from home. These provide "bridges—transitional learning experiences which aid parents in adapting themselves to postparental life" (Deutscher, "Socialization for Postparental Life," p. 435). Act soon to prepare for the empty nest. Let your children have times away from you, on their own. Increase the length of these times as they get older. The "honeymoon" atmosphere of a childless weekend may be a real spark for your marriage, and your children too will have an enriching experience.

"These 'rehearsals' are not as difficult as 'opening night'—the real and permanent departure of the children which will come later. They are defined as temporary and are broken by regular visits home or the expectation that the children will at some time again return to live at home. But the 'temporary' can gradually shift into the permanent without any traumatic transition" (Deutscher, "Socialization for Postparental Life," p. 435).

One mother said, "The breaking point is when your children go away to college. After that you grow used to it. By the time they get married you're used to the idea of their being away and adjust to it." A father commented on his daughter's readiness for marriage: "Yes, I thought she was ready. She had already gone through five years of college and two years working." For another mother, military service was the bridge. "We had gotten used to just being by ourselves while he was in the Navy." Another reacted this way when asked how she was doing now that all the children were gone, "Oh, I don't know. I was just too busy to be bothered about anything."

In-Laws Are In

The departure of a child from home often is due to his or her marriage, which brings our attention to another cultural myth: "In-laws are horrible, meddling people." Of course, when your children marry, you become an in-law, and although the label "father-in-law" doesn't have a particular connotation, few women feel that the label "mother-in-law" is complimentary.

Most of us who are in-laws have been so repulsed by the negative in-law stereotype that we bend over backwards not to cause any trouble. Someone has suggested that "mother-in-law jokes and stereotypes teach the future mother-in-law what kind of behavior is not acceptable." One woman said, "As soon as my youngsters were born I made up my mind that I was not going to be a mother-in-law like you read about."

The marriage of your children can be a trauma if for some reason you do not approve of the match. A different sort of crisis is the child who doesn't marry. If there were ever a dangerous and damaging stereotype, it is that people who don't marry have something wrong with them. It has caused far more grief than all the empty nest and in-law myths combined.

The solution to this crisis is to *affirm* that God has a plan for your child. *Trust* that He can work it out with your child, and *commit* yourself to noninterference. Affirm that God's plan for your child can be rewarding even if it does not include marriage. If you have further questions about this subject, I suggest that you read the book in this series on single adults and the church.

And God Made Grandparents

The next mark of your aging, after your children leave home and marry, is that they have children. You become a grandparent. In most cases, becoming a grandparent is hardly a crisis. It is' probably the most welcome sign of aging there is. "Grandchildren are the crown of old men" (Prov. 17:6). Ruth Shonle Cavan says, "Women especially visualize themselves as grandparents before a child is born and eagerly await the birth of a grandchild so they may express the grandmother self-image in an appropriate role" (Ruth Shonle Cavan, "Self and Role Adjustment During Old Age," *Family Roles and Interaction: An Anthology*, p. 461).

There are many people today who become grandparents in their early or middle forties, and some are great-grandparents in their sixties. It is not so unusual to see pictures of five generations together. This is due to the fact that there are many early marriages, and also that people live longer than in previous times. It brings together a wider span of generations living at the same time.

The value of grandparents should not be underestimated. Grandparents frequently have more influence per time invested than do parents because of their unique relationship to their grandchildren. Grandparents are usually more relaxed than parents.

This makes them approachable. They concentrate on giving love (sometimes called spoiling) without the necessity of meting out discipline. Their time with their grandchildren is usually better planned and more intentional than parents' time. All of this adds up to what some social scientists have called the "grandfather phenomenon." Children catch more of their grandparents' perspective on life than that of their parents. This can be a comfort if you are wondering about the effects of how your children are raising your grandchildren, and you may consider it a call to action to make the most of your time when you are with them.

Since becoming a grandfather, I have become aware of two things—what I can give and what I missed. Having seen my mistakes in fathering and having learned a bit since then, I want to pass on to my grandson a richer experience than I was able to give my sons.

I did not enjoy my children as I wish I could have because of time absorption in earning a living. I missed some of the emotional satisfaction that I'm finding with my grandson.

Retired or Tired?

Retirement is the fulcrum of the graying years. Unlike the emptying of the nest, the crisis of retirement is no myth. The decisions pile up at this time of life, just as they did at the start of marriage. In many ways, they are the mirror image of those early decisions. The practical concerns can be overwhelming at the time of retirement, but the emotional adjustment is a crippler for those who do not take decisive action.

If career success has been life's number one priority, the emptiness of such a priority will become evident at retirement. Your worth as an individual should not be based on your ability to perform your job or your ego will collapse when you retire and can no longer work in the same way as before.

Cavan identifies four things that damage a man's self-image when he stops working at retirement. "First, the means of carrying out the social role disappears: the man is a lawyer without a case, a bookkeeper without books, a machinist without tools. Second, he is excluded from his group of former co-workers; as an isolated person he may be completely unable to function in his former role. Third, as a retired person, he begins to find a different evaluation of himself in the minds of others from the evaluation he had as an employed person. . . . He is done for, an old-timer, old-fashioned, on the shelf. Fourth, he cannot accept this new valuation of himself for several reasons. He has had the old self-image for so many years that it has become part and parcel of himself. . . . Any movement toward solving the conflict is made difficult because the new self-image offered by those around him is of lower valuation than his internalized self-image" (Cavan, "Self and Role in Adjustment During Old Age," *Family Roles and Interaction: An Anthology,* pp. 462-463).

This analysis sounds almost hopeless but is not. Start by affirming the opportunities that come with retirement. Time is probably the chief commodity of retirement and can either be a millstone about your neck or the wealth for which you have been longing all of your life.

Look for opportunities that affirm your worth and value as a person. These may be contacts with people you have cultivated over the years either professionally, through your church, or as friends. Opportunities may arise from a special knowledge or skill you can provide that is of value to other people. Perhaps you can pursue a secret dream you've had, a foreign trip, a book to write, a craft to learn, a political office, a building project, or a ministry to support. These ideas may not appeal to you, and may even seem corny and unsatisfying. That's all right; take steps to find your own, and God will lead you. You need only one thing that affirms you as a person of worth to make all the difference.

When planning for your retirement, don't settle for something just to keep you busy. That would be a hollow victory and would not answer your need for dignity. Patiently search for an opportunity that will allow you to express your own personal meaning and significance.

The question of worth and self-image is foundational to the crisis of retirement, but the solution is found largely in acting on the practical level.

Your Retirement Plan

Ideally, you should plan for retirement. Counseling is available in most areas for emotional and pragmatic retirement problems. Seeking such assistance can be most helpful if you are stalemated in your retirement planning.

A retirement plan is usually thought of as something an insurance man tries to sell you or an item for negotiation in a union
contract. To be sure, money is a major element in retirement planning. Many of the problems of retirement hinge on the change of
financial circumstances. Several other issues are important too,
and no matter how old you are, you can commit yourself to prepare a retirement plan.

Finances
Financial planning is a sensible starting point. Study Social Security and find out what benefits are available to you, how much
retirement income it will provide, what limitations it places on
your other income during retirement, and what pension benefits
are available to you through your union or job.

You should also consider your life insurance and investments.
Since your need for life insurance changes as you grow older,
you will want to discover if you can use any of the value you may
have accumulated for retirement income. If you have made investments over the years, you may consider converting them to a
form that can become retirement income if necessary. Discover
what changes retirement will make in your health insurance. You
may need a new program.

Leaving the Job
An important part of the retirement plan that is often neglected
is how you will leave your job. Perhaps your company has a
mandatory retirement age. Being "put out to pasture" on your
birthday, may be a blow to your ego, but you can share in deciding on your terminal date in most cases. If a mandatory age has
not been set for retirement, you will need to decide when you will
finish up these responsibilities. Deciding this yourself instead of
being asked to leave can be a big boost to your morale. If you
don't incur a pension penalty, you may wish to leave a little early
to get a headstart on your new life. If you feel you have something
to contribute, however, and the company agrees, you may wish to
delay retirement. A conflict with your employer over a retirement
date can be deeply distressing. If you take the initiative and act
first, you may be able to avoid a hassle.

When your old job is taken care of, you need to plan what you will do when you retire. Of course, it is most useful to start well in advance of actual retirement. Try out some of the things you have in mind beforehand to help remove the dread of the idle days that retirement can mean. You may need or wish to supplement your other income sources with a job. Write out, with your spouse, a list of all the things you think you could do, either separately or together, that would bring in some income. Everything from a second career to selling your handcrafts should be carefully considered.

Organized Leisure or Second Career

A well-planned retirement usually has one of two emphases: organized leisure or a second career. The two often are mixed in varying degrees at different times during retirement. Certain military and civil service personnel have the opportunity for quite early retirement with a decent pension and the pursuit of an active second career, sometimes in the same field. I have many retired military friends doing well in a second career.

Early retirement can make possible a second career in various kinds of Christian service. Many retired, highly skilled military officers are making a significant contribution to well-known Christian organizations. Two men who are civil servants are planning for this in the near future. One has only one child who lives in another part of the country. He will be able to retire with a rather sizeable portion of his pension before he is 60 years old. He and his wife plan to move closer to their child and grandchildren, and he can take a low-paying job in a clerical or warehouse position for a Christian organization. The other will be able to retire when he is 60 with his full pension. He is thinking of moving to an area with a small rural church which needs help. He would serve as a business manager, visitation officer, and general errand runner to help the entire congregation become more vital.

A second career may fill the time with interesting activity and provide helpful income, but its primary value is an avenue for worthwhile participation in life. The late Paul Tournier wrote that a second career "can be voluntary, it can be paid, but without any compulsory relationship between earnings and output. It has nothing to do, therefore, with the idea of a second job, which so many pensioners accept perforce, in order to better their financial position." He described a second career as a "plant whose seed has been sown in the midst of a person's active life, which has taken root, which has developed tentatively at first, but which bears all its fruits in retirement" (Paul Tournier, *Learning to Grow Old,* New York: Harper and Row, 1971, p. 133).

Leisure is another emphasis of a planned retirement. It is not at odds with a second career nor with occasional work projects. In fact, everyone has some leisure time whether or not they are retired. If you are at the peak of frenzy over career and family, the leisure of retirement may seem ideal. Once you are there, however, it can easily become a burden of boredom, loneliness, uselessness, and frustration. Whether it is the major emphasis of your retirement or simply a fill-in around a second career, the leisure time of your retirement deserves to be planned.

Travel and hobbies are the most commonly thought of leisure activities for retirement. Travel, if you have the money and physical stamina for it, offers new experiences and encounters with new people. Some take a pilgrimage to the "old country" and find it exciting to discover their roots. Others find such a journey disappointing, for the reality doesn't measure up to what they had imagined.

Some hobbies can grow into full-time occupations, whether or not they are income producing, such as gardening, cabinetmaking, and art. Others will only fill in around the edges of life. Few people can build a new life around stamp collecting or gourmet cooking. If your hobby becomes your second career, you will need other leisure activities to give you a break.

All of this rests on having a leisure activity plan for retirement. Sit down with your spouse on several occasions to develop and adjust your plan. Start well ahead of your retirement date and keep current with periodic conferences. List activities you each like to do with your leisure. Then add the things you like to do together. Break them into categories of those that could become major emphasis and those that will always be fill-ins. Rank them according to what is most appealing to you, select three or four, then assign times to certain events. Some may be things you will want to do over and over again like a weekly swim or a monthly concert.

Roles and Life-style

Retirement brings a change of life-style that affects your marriage. The whole pattern of your relationship is altered. Once you spent evenings, weekends, and vacations together. Your times together were intermittent and special. In retirement, you are together most of the time and this can put a great deal of stress on a marriage, particularly if the husband is struggling to find an identity to replace the self-image he lost when he retired.

When the retired husband finds himself without his usual means of expression of his self-conception through his work role, he may try to work out a new role at home, without materially changing his self-image. Like a bull in a china shop, we have a man whose self-conception tells him to be competent, decisive, and productive, electing to express this self in a situation in which the available roles are already filled by his wife, who within her home, visualizes herself as competent, decisive, and productive. The husband's entrance into the situation tends to create tension in the former coordination between himself and his wife with respect both to their self-images and their roles. The husband sometimes attempts to express his superior status by assuming the decision-making roles in the home; or he may become a self-appointed expert, either criticizing or making suggestions regarding the way in which his wife manages the home. In thus attempting to give expression to his self-conception, he threatens his wife's image of herself. The wife is not opposed to having help in her housekeeping, but her self-conception calls for subordinates who take directions from her. Here, then, is a serious conflict between husband and wife in terms of their self-conceptions and roles. The problem is not one of what housework the husband will do, but of how the self-conceptions of husband and wife will be readjusted (Cavan, "Self and Role Adjustment During Old Age, *Family Roles and Interaction,* p. 465).

The solution to this conflict is immediate action. The principles are the same as for solving any marital difficulty, only now you are in unfamiliar territory because of the increased time you have together. Start by affirming that your time together is a gift from

God. Welcome the opportunities for deepening your love relationship. Take special delight in doing things for each other.

Each of you must take definitive action to make this work. The wife must openly welcome her husband's participation in the household tasks that have been hers alone all these years. She should be patient with his criticism and suggestions. The husband must recognize he is invading his wife's territory and not try to take over. He should let her give him directions and restrain his urge to change it all around and criticize or make suggestions. If he thinks he has something particularly constructive to offer, he should be very tactful about the time and way in which the suggestion is offered and make sure she understands it in terms of benefit to her, not just as one of his ideas.

A couple should take advantage of the opportunity for increased marital fellowship during retirement, but they need also to affirm the validity and value of separate activities. They need time apart to appreciate their times together and should commit themselves to encouraging each other to have their own interests. They should cultivate a few things to do and people to do them with that do not require their spouse. Unpleasant as it is to consider, this may be the little extra needed to help them through the period of bereavement when their spouse dies. But more important, it will make their marriage better now. It is especially important for the husband to develop an area of life where he can feel "competent, decisive, and productive" separate from his wife.

Sex Too?

A word about sex after retirement is important while thinking about the marriage relationship. In Marabel Morgan's *Total Joy,* one woman said, "Well, all of that's kid stuff. We're more mature than that." Then two months later her husband said, "I'm leaving you because you've been like a mother around here instead of my wife" (Marabel Morgan, *Total Joy,* Old Tappan: Revell, 1977, p. 132). No more parenting. This is the time to live marriage to the hilt and keep yourselves attractive to each other. Husbands report that they are looking to their wives as a confidant more now than at any other time of their lives. This intimacy can and should include an active sex life.

Though you might slow down, there is no reason to stop your

sexual relationship. Modern sex research indicates that you must "use it or lose it." You have learned a lot about each other in 40 or 50 years of marriage. Now you have the opportunity to use it for the joy of your partner, which will in turn be a delight for you. Husband and wife are more together in their sexual cycles at this time of life than at any time previously. They can enjoy each other with greater depth and intimacy.

Retirement may be the event that prompts the practical decisions and tangible crises, but the driving force behind it is the aging process. We are all growing old; it's just that some of us got there first. Unfortunately, those who are lagging behind in youth think they are immune and that old age is a chosen sin or at least an irresponsibly contracted disease. Some cultures venerate age to the point of the idolatry of ancestor worship. But our culture, at best, ignores the old. At worst, it treats them as a liability to be disposed of as painlessly, inexpensively, and quickly as possible.

The Bible takes a different perspective. An elder held a respected position in ancient Israel and in the primitive church. Abraham's epitaph does not sound like the frustrated old people we see in our society. "And Abraham breathed his last and died in a ripe old age, an old man and satisfied with life; and he was gathered to his people" (Gen. 25:8).

What a goal! To be an "old man and satisfied with life." So many enemies of satisfaction exist for old people: loneliness, isolation, boredom, dependence, disrespect, failing health. The outer conditions may be beyond your control, but you can act to bring satisfaction to your own life as you grow old. "Therefore, we do not lose heart, but though our outer man is decaying, yet our inner man is being renewed day by day" (2 Cor. 4:16).

12

King of Terrors

Other crises may be predictable and common, but death is inescapable and universal. It is the dark fear lurking behind our other fears, yet it promises release, and for some, escape from those fears. Concern with death permeates the thinking of the human race.

Joshua and David spoke of their impending deaths as "going the way of all the earth" (Josh. 23:14; 1 Kings 2:2). The writer of Hebrews (9:27) noted that "it is appointed for men to die once." It may come early or suddenly, slowly or in old age. But death will come. The mystery of death is so profound that no one can adequately prepare for it. No one can fully grasp or explain its significance, yet everyone will experience it.

Principles that have been helpful in dealing with other crises fade into feeble meaninglessness in the face of death. The principles of Act—affirm, commit, trust—are no exception. For in a real sense, when death strikes, there is nothing left to do. Nevertheless, the passage through grief is not an uncharted, trackless wilderness.

People take one of three approaches to that journey through grief. One is *hopelessness and despair*. In his advice to Job, Bildad echoed this sense of hopelessness when he called death "the king of terrors" (Job 18:14).

Job's answer to Bildad was a marked contrast—one of *confidence and hope*. In the face of doubt, disaster, and disease, Job said, "I know that my Redeemer lives, and at last He will take His stand on the earth. Even after my skin is flayed, yet without my flesh I shall see God" (Job 19:25-26).

131

The third approach is *false hope*. People will clutch at the thinnest thread of hope when confronted with death. For instance, interest in reincarnation is growing. What began as an academic study of people who have had resuscitation experiences has become a popular craze. I am not in a position to evaluate the experiences of those who have been revived after clinical "deaths." But I fear that some are grasping at these things as a hope for a universally pleasant existence after death. *Any hope that is not founded on the redemptive work of Christ is a false hope.*

My purpose in this chapter is not so much to argue that Christ offers the only hope in the face of death, which He does, as to help Christians learn healthy grief as God's way of coping with the crisis of death.

Paul had a similar purpose when he wrote to the Thessalonian church. They were anxiously awaiting the return of Jesus. But it was taking longer than they anticipated. People who fully expected to be personal witnesses of His coming were starting to die. The church was concerned about the state of these who were dying. So Paul wrote, "But we do not want you to be uninformed, brethren, about those who are asleep, that you may not grieve, as do the rest who have no hope. For if we believe that Jesus died and rose again, even so God will bring with Him those who have fallen asleep in Jesus. . . . Therefore comfort one another with these words" (1 Thes. 4:13-14, 18).

The Christian's Hope

Grief is necessary when dealing with death. Jesus even grieved at the death of His friend Lazarus just moments before He raised him from the grave (John 11:33-38). Hope does not banish grief but tempers it. Hope transforms grief from defeat to power and victory: "Death is swallowed up in victory. O death, where is your victory? O death, where is your sting?" (1 Cor. 15:54-55)

The hope of the Christian is unique. The Bible presents a picture of the future life that is distinct from that of all human religions. It is not the assuming of a new identity as in reincarnation or the loss of identity as in nirvana. It is not an ethereal, ghostlike haunting of this world or another. The Apostles' Creed describes this hope as "the resurrection of the body, and the life everlasting." The New Testament's major teaching on the resurrection of the body is found in 1 Corinthians 15. Paul tied the resurrection of Jesus directly to the resurrection of His saints. He promises bodies and a life like that of Jesus after His resurrection. This is the hope that gives healing power to grief. "For our earthly bodies, the ones we have now that can die, must be transformed into heavenly bodies that cannot perish but will live forever" (1 Cor. 15:53, LB).

Close Encounters

You may not have thought much about death; many people have not. Someone you know may have died and you may have attended funerals, but you may not have had an encounter with a dying person. When it comes, the depth of the hope in the resurrection of the body will resound through your soul. Your first encounter with death may be one in which you witness an accident.

Jay Kesler, of Youth for Christ, had such a sobering experience:

> I saw the accident. A car carrying a load of kids had turned over and the car was upside down, the wheels still spinning. I pulled over and went from person to person seeing if I could do anything to help. There was one girl who had virtually nothing left of her face. She was crying, in terrible pain. I held her in my arms; there was nothing else I could do. I found myself praying, "God, take her now." And He did take her; she died right there while I watched her.
>
> Thinking back over that experience still makes me feel frightened. But why? Why was it such a strong experience for me? I knew then and I know now that people die on the highways every day. I hear the reports on the radio, and it doesn't affect me at all. I certainly didn't know that particular girl, she hadn't meant anything to me. The only difference between her death and the thousands I hear about every year was that I happened to be there when it happened. Yet it moved me in a way few things in life do.
>
> The reason that's so is that it made the reality of my own death much more real. It could have been me; my car could have been the one flipped upside down, and I

could have been the person crying and trying to gasp a few last breaths. Of course, I'd known that all along. I know there's a reason I have to buy car insurance just like everyone else. I'm not Superman, and statistically I'm as likely to die as the next person. But that girl, whose name I don't even know, brought death out of the realm of statistics and obituary pages, and into bone and blood. For quite a while after that experience I couldn't ignore the fact that I, Jay Kesler, was going to die. It was a frightening realization (Jay Kessler and Tim Stafford, *Outside Disneyland* Waco: Word Books, 1977, pp. 21-22).

Death, unlike the other crises in this book, is nonreversible. Nothing can be done to return the deceased to life. You are left with trusting God for the resurrection. Nevertheless, the work of grief must be completed. Others around you are participating in the same grief and some practical matters must be cared for, even if you do not feel like it. The needed action will only take you through grief, not around it.

Explaining Death to Children

When death strikes in a family, one of the most important considerations is explaining it to the children. This is necessary for them to work through their own grief, and it also helps us deal with our own feelings. After all, we are all just children when we meet the king of terrors.

Death is one of those crucial topics that parents should discuss with their children before a crisis arises, much like sex. Unfortunately, death, like sex, is something parents feel uncomfortable with and avoid discussing with their children. Yet death is a part of life. Its presence is everywhere, so parents have many opportunities for talking about it with their children. The Bible is not squeamish about death as we are, and if you are reading the Bible with your family, you will read about the deaths of both good and evil people. You will read about death as the penalty for sin, as a result of wars, old age, illness. You will read of the deaths of young and old—and sometimes of God's reaction to death. Don't just read past these things. Stop and ask your children questions such as, "How do you think Abraham and Isaac felt when Sarah died?" (Gen. 23 and 24:67—25:1) "Why

did Jesus cry just before He raised Lazarus from the grave?"
"Why was Simeon ready to die?" (Luke 2:29)

Families with pets or those who live on a farm will be acquainted
with the deaths of animals. A well-known person or someone in
your church may die. These are opportunities for preparing for
death when the emotions can be felt but without the same pain as
a death in the immediate family. You can talk about the difference
between real and pretend death, the differences between natural,
accidental, and intentional death, and begin to cope with the feelings of grief that may emerge in these experiences. These are
important "teachable moments" that you can use to prepare your
children and yourself for unforeseen deaths.

You can plan for opportunities to discuss death in your family
as well. Certain books and even selected television programs deal
with death in a more profound and healthy way than the average
thriller. In fact, God in His grace seems frequently to send His
children opportunities to contemplate death shortly before someone close is to die. Don't cringe back from these experiences.
Accept them with thanks as gifts from a gracious God.

Two high school friends of one girl were killed in a car accident.
That prompted a good deal of discussion within the family about
death, how it comes, and its meaning. Her parents used this
experience as a significant opportunity to help her deal with her
grandfather's impending death.

When the grandfather died a few weeks later, the parents took
their daughter with them on the trip to the funeral. The whole
family had gathered, though they had never all been together in
that way since childhood. This teenage daughter observed a
number of things about her parents, herself, and her grandparents
from participating in this event. The esteem and love she felt for
her now deceased grandfather increased considerably at this time,
though she had usually thought of him as rather harsh when he
was alive. She gained an understanding and appreciation of her
father's relationship with his brothers as she saw them all staying
together for a few days in one house. Perhaps most significant
was the humanizing effect all of this had on her image of her
grandfather. She was present for the closing of the casket following
the funeral. She watched her father and her uncles share their
grief for their father, though they had all struggled with him con-

136 / CONQUERING FAMILY STRESS

siderably, even into adulthood. Perhaps the most moving, significant part of this experience for her was when her grandmother kissed her grandfather's body just before the casket was closed. She said that at that point she saw her grandfather not just as a grandpa, not even just as a father, but as a husband, a man, a lover, even though he was now well into his 70s.

The death of someone of the grandparent generation is not as shocking or difficult as when a younger person dies, but the grief is real. These family experiences can be quite warm and comforting as you remember together positive and realistic things from the past. This is an important part of affirming the value of the one who has died and coming to grips with your sense of loss. The process of remembering, though difficult and sorrowful, is an important part of the work of grief. These recollections become the "folklore" of the family that help establish a sense of identity and roots. To attempt to shelter children from the pain of grief at death is to cheat them out of developing a sense of pride and respect for their family background.

Children Often Have More Faith than Parents

The simple faith of a child often is a comfort to his or her parents. A child can accept "to be absent from the body, and to be present with the Lord" at face value. And that is a comfort of more immediacy than the final resurrection. One young mother received a long distance call in the middle of the night when she was alone with her three-year-old child. The caller told her that her mother had suddenly died. She just felt that she had to tell someone what had happened, so she went in to her daughter's bedroom, sat down beside her and said, "Sweetheart, Grandma has gone to be with Jesus." And the little girl sat up, so excited. She said, "Oh, Mommy, that's wonderful! Just think, Grandma is talking to Jesus right now. Oh, I'm so happy for Grandma."

Children wonder, as do adults, what it is like for a person who has died. They will ask, "What is heaven like?" Theologians have analyzed biblical data on heaven for centuries, but our curiosity remains unsatisfied. Read some of the books that have been written about heaven or use a concordance, topical Bible, and study Bible, to discover the Bible's own words about heaven with your family. Since this information is both symbolic and sketchy, you can let your imaginations roam in the spacious field of God's Word. Perhaps reading together books such as C. S. Lewis' *Chronicles of Narnia* will give you the opportunity as a family to imagine the glories God has waiting for His children.

Deaths of friends, grandparents, and other relatives can strike hard at a child but the loss of a sibling or parents is devastating. The closeness of the relationship brings an intensity of emotion that overwhelms. When a parent dies, the child may feel abandoned and helpless and others need to be ready with reliable support and help. The squabbles and stress of family living also generate guilt feelings when a family member dies. Children may believe that their anger "magically" killed the sibling or parent. These feelings deserve to be expressed and accepted.

The pain and bewilderment at a time like this debilitates children and adults alike. They need a sense of God's care for them and the deceased, but it comes gradually and gently. Lectures do not do the job. The Bible uses a variety of symbolic expressions to describe death, which can be helpful in dealing with our own grief as well as helping children with theirs. The late Donald Grey Barnhouse tells of his experience when his wife died:

"I was driving with my children to my wife's funeral where I was to preach the sermon. As we came into one small town there strode down in front of us a truck that came to stop before a red light. It was the biggest truck I ever saw in my life, and the sun was shining on it at just the angle that took its shadow and spread it across the snow on the field beside it.

"As the shadow covered that field, I said, 'Look, children, at that truck, and look at its shadow. If you had to be run over, which would you rather be run over by? Would you rather be run over by the truck or by the shadow?'

"My youngest child said, 'The shadow couldn't hurt anybody.'

"That's right," I continued, "and death is a truck, but the shadow is all that ever touches the Christian. The truck ran over the Lord Jesus. Only the shadow is gone over mother" (Donald Grey Barnhouse, *Eternity,* October 1977, p. 28).

Death of Your Spouse

The death of your spouse poses another entirely different set of questions. The person who has never imagined and wondered what would happen should their spouse die would be unusual indeed. Recollections of these thoughts may produce tremendous guilt. In almost every situation, the one left would suffer from feelings of inadequacy and desire to have shown more love. When a relationship has been strained or there has been a conflict of some sort immediately preceding the death of the spouse, guilt feelings can be unbearable. Death of a spouse also brings with it a great deal of anxiety for the future. When the breadwinner is the one who goes, financial security becomes an issue. When the housekeeper goes, particularly if there are still children at home, routine household care becomes a serious problem. Blended into all of this are the normal processes of grief and the realization of an oppressive loneliness.

For elderly couples, the death of the partner may be a relief coupled with a prayer for their own soon departure. Loneliness is a real crisis for these people. If they have been able to live independently by depending on each other, the death of one partner can stimulate the physical and social decline of the other. Younger people with active lives ahead of them feel the loss of a spouse more acutely at first, though they often adjust well. The couple with young children or even teenagers living at home when one partner dies face some of the hardest practical and emotional problems of death.

Death of Your Child
Parents are often plagued with guilt feelings at the death of a child, especially if there is some evidence of parental neglect involved.

Wife and husband often drift apart in the process of grieving for the loss of a child. They find they do not really share each other's grief. They need to talk, but have trouble talking to each other. Unless a healing occurs in their relationship, they may become so isolated from each other that they break up. Their marriage has proven unequal to the task of supporting them through the trauma of this tragedy.

Help from a Church
The emotional needs of couples who have lost children and of those whose spouses have died are similar. They need support that

continues for months past the funeral. They need to talk as they work through their grief. They cannot meet these needs themselves. In fact, they are usually so emotionally distressed that they will not seek out this sort of help for themselves. In many cases they are so vulnerable they are unable to discern who can be trusted with their grief. This is an opportunity for the church to minister to them.

The Redeemer Lutheran Church of Hinsdale, Illinois seeks to meet this need. It has made its facilities available for monthly meetings of Compassionate Friends, a nonsectarian "self-help group for parents who have suffered the death of an offspring." Loren and Marylue Getz of Winfield, Illinois, became active in the group when their son David died.

"There is a need to talk," Marylue said. "We had to have a place to express our feelings about the child who was part of our life. Friends who hadn't undergone the death of a child didn't seem to be able to share the grief.

Most people can't extend themselves beyond the time of the funeral. They become uncomfortable around them, uncertain of the proper response.

Some said, "Oh, it's a blessing." Marylue responds, "You just can't write off a loss that easily. I'm still trying to get reoriented to things I give my time to."

People don't come to Compassionate Friends for answers. Often, there are none.

"It's the spirit of acceptance, of real human understanding which touches members," she said. "Many who were struggling with personal and marital difficulties show healing over the months."

For the Getzes, it is the understanding of their marriage which made the continual contact with the church most valuable. "We continue to learn about ourselves," she said, referring to her husband and herself as part of the common exchange of views.

Still, healing is a lengthy process. The Getz family, with one 11-year-old son and another now seven, still mourn and celebrate David. Timetables differ, but many find five and six years lapsed time doesn't remove the melancholy. Anniversaries, birthdays and special holidays become times of remembered sorrow.

Marylue feels restless in the fall, which is the time of David's birth and death. Still, she approaches the message of her child's death with hope.

"It's one of the most deepening events in my life, and I want to grow from it," she said. Her family, especially the two younger sons, are encouraged to remember David. After being so involved with preserving David through his life of sickness, they preserve his special meaning for the family (*The Daily Journal,* Wheaton, Ill., October 19, 1977, p. 17).

The needs of those who have lost a child and those who have lost a spouse are not too different. Your church could offer some of the same kind of support as Compassionate Friends. Its biblical resource would be of great value as it provided a setting for Christians to explore and work through their grief. That solid spiritual foundation could also be a genuine outreach ministry in your community. The environment of accepting feelings of grief is primary. If your church does not have occasion to assume this sort of ministry on a formal basis, close friends can fulfill it in informal fellowship.

Advance Preparations

The Bible records several incidents of people making advance preparation for their own deaths. Two of the most notable are Moses (Num. 27:12-23) and David (1 Kings 2:1-10). They were concerned for the continuing leadership of the nation and took specific steps to insure that their responsibilities would be cared for when they died. A few things can be done in advance that will make death much easier to deal with on a practical level when it comes.

A great percentage of couples have never prepared a will, though a will determines how your property will be disposed of should you die. The importance of that is covered in the book on family finances in this series. But a few nonfinancial questions may be even more important. In preparing a will you will contact a lawyer and name trusted people to care for your estate. This process will help simplify things for you or your spouse should the other die first, and is absolutely essential should you die simultaneously.

If you have children, you will name guardians. Even if you

have very little in the way of wealth to be concerned with, providing trusted care for your children is worth the price of the will. Consider this carefully; your closest relatives or friends you first think of may not be the best choice. Think of who will raise your children as you would, instilling in them the same kinds of values you hold. Who will give your children the love that you are no longer able to provide?

Wills and other previous arrangements can care for a host of other things. You may wish to be an organ donor. Corneal transplants are particularly easy and helpful in bringing sight to someone who is blind. And some people have donated their bodies for study by medical schools and research institutions. I am not suggesting any particular plan for you, but these things need to be arranged for in advance, and your immediate family should be aware of your wishes.

Dying at Home

Medical technology has lengthened and, in many ways, improved our lives. It has tended, however, to make death impersonal: it cheats families of warm good-byes; it puts helpless people in sterile, unfamiliar surroundings during life's final stress. But this need not be a hindrance to those who plan ahead for impending deaths. Unless hospital care is absolutely necessary for medical treatment, I would suggest planning to die at home.

A friend of mine had his grandmother living with his family as he was growing up. When it became obvious that she was going to die, the family arranged to equip her room and care for her themselves. The family learned to care in a new and deeper sense. The grandmother had the comfort of feeling the love of her family in this care rather than just the professional but impersonal care of hospital staff. When she died, the family could be genuinely thankful for her release from pain. She was not denied any medical help, and she received and gave a priceless gift of love by dying at home.

Funeral Planning

Funerals can be, and frequently are, planned in advance. A single woman had been a missionary for a number of years but retired from active service when stricken by a rare disease that was ultimately fatal. She willed her body to medical research in hopes of helping others with the disease. She wrote out her entire funeral in advance and included it with her will. The funeral was held in her home church and planned as a celebration of victory and healing. Though the event was sad, even several years later, people in that church who were part of that funeral still talk about the confidence and faith they gained from it. They knew she was not present in the deceased body but was with the Lord.

I recently attended several funerals and observed that they have not really been very comforting. When a Christian is the deceased, talking about the resurrection of the dead is the biblical message of hope that every Christian can share. By planning ahead for your own funeral, you can make a positive and comforting statement to your friends and relatives who will attend. Most funeral homes have ways of making the basic arrangements in advance. This relieves your spouse and family of the burden of making expensive decisions when their judgment is impaired by grief.

One congregation offered an adult Sunday School elective on death and the group took a field trip to a mortuary. The funeral director explained how a funeral is handled from beginning to end. The people walked through the process as part of their tour and had opportunity to ask questions. A couple of years later the elderly father of one of the men in the group died. This man then told others who had been in the group how valuable that experience had been. He knew what to expect. He had already worked through in his mind some of the decisions before talking with the funeral director. The dry run, when he had not been emotionally involved, freed him to deal with his grief.

You can also prepare yourself emotionally for death: your own or someone else's. Study what the Bible has to say about death and the resurrection. Joe Bayly's book, *View from a Hearse,* is excellent. Secular works on death can be helpful as well, if they are measured against the Bible. Perhaps you could encourage your church to sponsor a seminar, film, or class on preparing for death. You may be surprised how popular it would be among Christians, as well as outsiders, if you were to publicize it.

Facing Your Own Death

One of the best-known secular students of death and dying is Elizabeth Kubler-Ross. Through her research with terminally ill patients, she has identified stages of grief that people go through when facing their own deaths. The experience of grieving for someone else is very similar. If you understand that these stages are part of the normal process of grief, you will not be so distressed when you experience them yourself. And you will have enough understanding not to belittle or scold someone else who experiences grief. These same emotional stages of grief are evidenced in encounters with death recorded in the Bible.

The first stage is denial. People can't believe they are to die or that their loved one has died. I think many of us had that feeling the first couple of days after President John Kennedy was shot. It seemed unreal. People kept saying to themselves, "It just can't be real. This must be a bad dream."

The second stage is resentment and anger. People ask "Why me? Why now?" The feelings of having good things cut off provoke outbursts of anger. This is a time of questioning God and raising doubts. Rational answers to these questions and doubts only provoke more anger. Acceptance of these as legitimate feelings help the person move through this stage. The questions must be asked or growth cannot occur.

The third stage is bargaining. People ask for a little more time. They struggle to stay alive for Christmas or until the distant son can return home. They may promise renewed devotion to God if He will let them live just a little longer. But the bargain doesn't bring renewal. (See 2 Kings 20 and Isaiah 38.)

The fourth stage is depression. The person retreats into silence. He may even ask previously welcome visitors to leave. Those mourning for others become withdrawn, lose their appetite, and suffer insomnia. They shun social contact. Those who would help need to be available at this time. They should not give up, or push and pry, even though they feel rejected. This darkness will pass, and their company will be welcome again.

The fifth and final stage is acceptance. This is not a giving up but a recognition and acceptance of reality. People have set their lives in order and cleared up troubled relationships in this stage. They are ready for the inevitable. At this stage, Christians have had profound ministries to medical personnel, other patients, friends, and relatives. Those who mourn for others are ready to reenter life in a normal but deeper way when they reach acceptance.

Elizabeth Kubler-Ross sometimes begins her lectures by saying, "In an audience like this certainly some are aware of being terminally ill. If you are terminal, raise your hand." Usually several people in the audience will reluctantly raise their hands. She responds by saying something like, "You are all terminal! Everyone must someday die." Some people do not come to the place of facing this as a human reality in their thinking. Others are afforded a brief opportunity for contemplating their death with the onset of some accident or swift illness. For many people, death gives a long advance warning, and they have greater opportunity to realize their own death.

You have had a vicarious encounter with the king of terrors by reading this chapter. Hopefully, you are better prepared to face death as a result. You may be called on to comfort someone who is grieving. You may have to mourn your parent, spouse, or child. You may be confronted with your own mortality.

When this happens there is nothing to do but cry and pray, and these are perhaps the most powerful things you can do. To say, "I care," gives more strength than all the medical, psychological, and theological explaining you can muster. People often seek comfort in the twenty-third Psalm in times of sorrow. Many of the psalms express the sorrow of God's people. You may find that reading them gives expression to the inner yearnings of grief.

As paradoxical as it seems, grief and hope go together. Hope draws its force from grief, for without sorrow there is no need for hope. It was Jesus, the "Man of sorrows and acquainted with grief," who said, "I am the resurrection and the life" (John 11:25).